FRENCH

Made Easy

Published By
Lotus Press Publishers & Distributors

FRENCH
Made Easy

Author
Md. Faizullah Khan
M. Phil. (JNU)
Assistant Professor (French)
Centre for European & Latin American Studies
Jamia Millia Islamia
New Delhi

Lotus PRESS
4735/22, Prakash Deep Building
Ansari Road, Darya Ganj,
New Delhi - 110002

Lotus Press : Publishers & Distributors
Unit No. 220, 2nd Floor, 4735/22, Prakash Deep Building,
Ansari Road, Darya Ganj, New Delhi- 110002
Ph.: 23280047, 98118-38000
• E-mail : lotuspress1984@gmail.com
www.lotuspress.co.in

French Made Easy

ISBN: 81-8382-186-3

Printed & Published by : **Lotus Press Publisher & Distributors,** New Delhi-02

TABLE OF CONTENTS

Introduction

This book has been professionally designed for students and tourists who want to learn French at their own pace. It aims at enabling learners to communicate in everyday situations that they may encounter in France and other Francophone countries. Comprising 14 thematic lessons, the book introduces the learners to practical themes such as greeting someone, meeting a stranger/a friend, introducing oneself, telling/asking for the time, talking about the weather, booking railway/air tickets, writing an informal letter and other such day to day activities. Each lesson deals with dialogues, vocabulary and grammar in a simple and concise manner. In addition to these carefully structured lessons, an additional glossary of some of the most common words has been given at the end of the book for quick reference for the learners. To help the learners learn how to pronounce French sounds appropriately, the pronunciation of each French word/expression/sentence used in this book is shown with the help of phonetic transcriptions. However, for the learners who are not familiar with phonetic transcription, the approximate sound of each phonetic symbol is shown through English words in the following pages.

Md Faizullah Khan

Phonetic Transcription

To help the learners learn how to pronounce French sounds, the pronunciation of each French word/expression/sentence used in this book is presented with the support of International Phonetic Alphabet. However, for the learners who are not familiar with the International Phonetic Alphabet, the approximate sound of each symbol is shown through English words in the following table.

PHONETIC SYMBOLS	SOUNDS IN ENGLISH

Vowels

[i]	tree
[e]	say, net
[ɛ]	bat
[a]	task
[ɔ]	pot
[o]	go
[u]	bull, cool
[y]	tube, new
[ø]	lieu
[œ]	shut
[ə]	enter

Nasal Vowels

[ɛ̃]	bank
[ã]	dance
[ɔ̃]	bond
[œ̃]	burnt

Consonants

[p]	pot
[b]	bank
[f]	fan
[v]	five
[k]	cut, king
[g]	gun
[t]	barista
[d]	they
[s]	say
[ʃ]	shut
[z]	zebra
[ʒ]	pleasure
[l]	luck
[r]	room
[m]	man
[n]	man
[ŋ]	parking
[ɲ]	onion

Semi-Vowels

[j]	yes
[ɥ]	twinkle
[w]	quantity

Abbreviations

The following abbreviations have been used in this book:

n.	noun
adj.	adjective
v.	verb
m./mas.	masculine
f./fem.	feminine
adv.	adverbs
prep.	preposition
sing.	singular
pl.	plural

Lesson 0

Alphabet *L'alphabet*

Capital Letters	Small Letters	Pronunciation
A	a	[a]
B	b	[be]
C	c	[se]
D	d	[de]
E	e	[ə]
F	f	[ɛf]
G	g	[ʒe]
H	h	[aʃ]
I	i	[i]
J	j	[ʒi]
K	k	[ka]
L	l	[ɛl]
M	m	[ɛm]
N	n	[ɛn]
O	o	[o]
P	p	[pe]
Q	q	[ky]
R	r	[ɛr]

S	s	[ɛs]
T	t	[te]
U	u	[y]
V	v	[ve]
W	w	[dubləwe]
X	x	[iks]
Y	y	[igrɛk]
Z	z	[zɛd]

ACCENTS LES ACCENTS

Accents		**Examples**	**Pronunciation**
.	Accent aigu	é	[e]
`	Accent grave	è	[ɛ]
		à	[a]
		ù	[u]
ˆ	Accent circonflexe/ chapeau	ê	[ɛ]
		î	[i]
¨	Thréma	ï	[i]
ç	Cédille	ç	[s]

NUMBERS	LES NOMBRES
0	zéro [zero]
1	un [œ̃]
2	deux [dø]
3	trois [trwa]
4	quatre [katr]
5	cinq [s ɛ̃k]
6	six [sis]
7	sept [set]
8	huit [ɥit]
9	neuf [nœf]
10	dix [dis]
11	onze [ɔ̃z]
12	douze [duz]
13	treize [trɛz]
14	quatorze [kat ɔrz]

15	quinze [k ɛ̃z]
16	seize [sɛz]
17	dix-sept [disɛt]
18	dix-huit [diz ɥit]
19	dix-neuf [diznœf]
20	vingt [v ɛ̃]
21	vingt et un [v ɛ̃te œ̃]
22	vingt-deux [v ɛ̃ dø]
23	vingt-trois [v ɛ̃ trwa]
24	vingt-quatre [v ɛ̃ katr]
25	vingt-cinq [v ɛ̃ s ɛ̃k]
26	vingt-six [v ɛ̃t sis]
27	vingt-sept [v ɛ̃t sɛt]
28	vingt-huit [v ɛ̃t ɥ it]
29	vingt-neuf [v ɛ̃t nœf]

30	trente [trãt]
31	trente et un [trãte œ̃]
40	quarante [karãt]
41	quarante et un [karãte œ̃]
50	cinquante [s ɛ̃kãt]
51	cinquante et un [s ɛ̃kãte œ̃]
60	soixante [swasãt]
61	soixante et un [swasãte œ̃]
70	soixante-dix [swasãt dis]
71	soixante et onze [swasãte ɔ̃z]
80	quatre vingts [katrə v ɛ̃]
81	quatre-vingt-un [katrə v ɛ̃t œ̃]
90	quatre-vingt-dix [katrə v ɛ̃ dis]
91	quatre-vingt-onze [katrə v ɛ̃ ɔ̃z]
97	quatre-vingt-dix-sept [katrəv ɛ̃ disɛt]
100	cent [sã]

101	cent un [sã œ̃]
200	deux cents [dø sã]
500	cinq cents [s ɛ̃k sã]
1000	mille [mil]
1900	mille neuf cents [mil nœf sã]
1000000	un million [œ̃milj ɔ̃]
1000000000	un milliard [œ̃miljar]

Lesson 1

How to greet someone — *Comment saluer quelquun*

Mr. Thomas: Good Morning, Madam	M. Thomas: Bonjour, madame. [bɔ̃ʒur madam]
Mrs. Vincent: Good Morning, Sir.	Mme. Vincent: Bonjour, monsieur. [bɔ̃ʒur məsjø]
Mr. Thomas: Good Afternoon, Madam.	M. Thomas: Bonjour, madame. [bɔ̃ʒur madam]
Mrs. Vincent: Good Afternoon, Sir.	Mme. Vincent: Bonjour, monsieur. [bɔ̃ʒur məsjø]
Mr. Thomas: Good Evening, Madam.	M. Thomas: Bonsoir, madame. [bɔ̃swar madam]
Mrs. Vincent: Good Evening, Sir.	Mme. Vincent: Bonsoir, monsieur. [bɔ̃swar məsjø]

Sophie: Hello, Shafaque.	Sophie: Bonjour, Shafaque [bɔ̃ʒur ʃəfək]
Shafaque: Hello, Sophie	Shafaque: Bonjour, Sophie. [bɔ̃ʒur sofi]
Sophie: Hi, Thierry.	Sophie: Salut, Thierry. [saly tjɛri]
Thierry: Hi, Sophie.	Thierry: Salut Sophie. [saly sofi]
Sophie: Good Night, Thierry.	Sophie: Bonne nuit, Thierry. [bɔnnɥi tjɛri]
Thierry: Good Night, Sophie.	Thierry: Bonne nuit, Sophie. [bɔnnɥi sofi]
Mr. Thomas: Good Bye, Madam.	M. Thomas: Au revoir, madame. [ɔ rəvwar madam]
Mrs. Vincent: Good Bye, Sir.	Mme. Vincent: Au revoir, monsieur. [ɔ rəvwar məsjø]
Sophie: Bye, Thierry.	Sophie: Salut, Thierry. [saly tjɛri]
Thierry: Bye, Sophie.	Thierry: Salut, Sophie. [saly sofi]

See you soon.	A bien tôt. [a bjɛ̃to]
See you in a moment.	A tout à l.heure. [a tuta lœr]
See you tomorrow.	A demain. [a dmɛ̃]
See you on Monday.	A lundi. [a lœ̃di]
See you later.	A plus tard. [a ply tar]

Singular	***Plural***
Monsieur [məsjø]	Messieurs [mesjø]
Madame [madam]	Mesdames [medam]
Mademoiselle [madmwazɛl]	Mesdemoiselles [medmwazɛl]

Abbreviations

Monsieur	M.
Madame	Mme.
Mademoiselle	Mlle.

Vocabulaire	***Vocbulary***
le jour (n.m.) [lə ʒur]	day
le matin (n.m.) [le mətɛ̃]	morning
l'après -midi (n.m.) [laprɛmidi]	afternoon
le soir (n.m.) [lə swar]	evening
la nuit (n.f.) [la nɥ i]	night
bon (adj. m.) [bɔ̃]	good
bonne (adj. f.) [bɔn]	good

Lesson 2

Meetings — *Les rencontres*

Meeting a stranger

Mr. Singh: Hello!	M. Singh: Bonjour! [bɔ̃ʒur]
Mr. Vincent: Hello!	M. Vincent: Bonjour! [bɔ̃ʒur]
Mr. Singh: Are you from France?	M. Singh: Vous venez de la France ? [vu vəne də la frɑ̃s]
Mr. Vincent: No, I am from Canada.	M. Vincent: Non, je viens du canada. [nɔ̃ ʒə vjɛ̃ dy kanada]
Mr. Singh: What is your name?	M. Singh: Comment vous appelez-vous ? [kɔmɑ̃ vu zaple vu]
Mr. Vincent: My name is Vincent.	M. Vincent: Je m'appelle Vincent. [ʒe mapɛl vɛ̃sɑ̃]

Mr. Singh: Where do you live in Canada?

M. Singh: Où habitez-vous au Canada?
[u abite vu o kanada]

Mr. Vincent: I live in Montreal.

M. Vincent: j'habite à Montréal.
[ʒabita mɔ̃real]

Mr. Singh: What do you do?

M. Singh: Quelle est votre profession?
[kɛlɛ vɔtr prɔfɛsjɔ̃]

Mr. Vincent: I am a professor.

M. Vincent: Je suis professeur.
[ʒə sɥi prɔfɛsœr]

Mr. Singh: Are you married?

M. Singh: Vous êtes marié?
[vuʒɛt marje]

Mr. Vincent: No, I am a bachelor.

M. Vincent: Non, Je suis célibataire.
[nɔ̃ʒc sɥi selibatɛr]

Meeting your superior/someone older to you

Paul: Hello, Sir.

Paul: Bonjour, monsieur.
[[bɔ̃ʒur məsjø]

Mr. Girard: Hello, Paul.

M. Girard: Bonjour, Paul.
[bɔ̃ʒur pɔl]

Paul: How are you?	Paul: Comment allez-vous? [kɔmãtale vu]
Mr. Girard: I am fine, and you?	M. Girard: Je vais bien. Et vous? [ʒə ve bjɛ̃e vu]
Paul: Very fine. Thank you.	Paul: Très bien. Merci. [trɛ bjɛ̃ mɛrsi]

Meeting a friend/someone younger to you

Paul: Hi Pierre.	Paul: Salut, Pierre. [saly pjɛr]
Pierre: Hi Paul. How is life?	Pierre: Salut, Paul. Ça va? [saly pɔl sa va]
Paul: Fine, and You?	Paul: Ça va. Et toi? [sa va e twa]
Pierre: Very fine.	Pierre: Très bien. [trɛ bjɛ̃]

Vocabulaire	*Vocabulary*
la profession (n.f.) [la prɔfɛsjɔ̃]	profession
le professeur (n.m.) [lə prɔfɛsœr]	professor
l'ami (n.m.) [lami]	friend (male)
l'amie (n.f.) [lami]	friend (female)
marié (adj. m.) [marje]	married (man)
mariée (adj. f.) [marje]	married (woman)
célibataire (adj. f.) [selibatɛr]	bachelor
bien (adv.) [bjɛ̃]	well, fine
très (adv.) [trɛ]	very
venir (v) [vənir]	to come
s'appeler (v) [saple]	to call oneself
habiter (v) [abite]	to live
être (v) [ɛtr]	to be
aller (v) [ale]	to go

Grammaire — Grammar

Pronoms sujets — Subject pronouns

Pronoms sujets	Subject pronouns
je [ʒə]	I
tu [ty]	you
il [il]	he
elle [ɛl]	she
nous [nu]	we
vous [vu]	you (formal, plural)
ils [il]	they
elles [ɛl]	they (feminine)

Conjugation of irregular verbs in 'présent'

être

je suis [ʒəsɥi]	I am
tu es [ty ɛ]	you are
il est [ilɛ]	he is
elle est [ɛlɛ]	she is
nous sommes [nu sɔm]	we are
vous êtes [vuzɛt]	you are
ils sont [il sɔ̃]	they are
elles sont [ɛl sɔ̃]	they are

Examples:

Je suis acteur. [ʒə sɥizaktœr]	I am an actor.
Je suis actrice. [ʒə sɥizaktris]	I am an actress.
Tu es acteur. [ty ɛ aktœr]	You are an actor.
Tu es actrice. [ty ɛ aktris]	You are an actress.

Il est acteur. [il ɛtaktœr]	He is an actor.
Elle est actrice. [ɛl ɛtaktris]	She is an actress.
Nous sommes acteur. [nu sɔmzaktœr]	We are actors.
Nous sommes actrice. [nu sɔmzaktris]	We are actresses.
Vous êtes acteur (s) Vous êtes actrice (s)	You are actor (s) You are actress (es)
Ils sont acteurs. [il sɔ̃taktœr]	They are actors.
Elles sont actrices. [ɛl sɔ̃taktris]	They are actresses.

aller

je vais [ʒə ve]	I go/I am going
tu vas [ty va]	you go/you are going
il va [il va]	he goes/he is going
elle va [ɛl va]	she goes/she is going
nous allons [nuzalɔ̃]	we go/we are going
vous allez [vu zale]	you go/you are going
ils vont [il vɔ̃]	they go/they are going

elles vont [ɛl vɔ̃]	they go/they are going

❖ The verb 'aller' takes the preposition ' à ' when it is followed by the name of a place and it takes 'chez' when followed by the name of a person or a personal pronoun.

Examples:

Je vais à paris. [ʒəve a pari]	I go to Paris/ I am going to Paris.
Je vais chez Paul. [ʒə ve ʃe pɔl]	I go to Paul's place/ I am going to Paul's place.
Tu vas à Paris. [ty va a pari]	You go to Paris/ You are going to Paris.
Tu vas chez Paul. [ty va ʃe pɔl]	You go to Paul's place/ You are going to Paul's place.
Tu vas chez lui. [ty va ʃelɥi]	You go to his place/ You are going to his place.

venir

je viens [ʒə vjɛ̃]	I come/I am coming
tu viens [ty vjɛ̃]	you come/you are coming
il vient [il vjɛ̃]	he comes/he is coming

elle vient [ɛl vjɛ̃]	she comes/she is coming
nous venons [nu vənɔ̃]	we come/we are coming
vous venez [vu vəne]	you come/you are coming
ils viennent [il vjɛn]	they come/they are coming
elles viennent [ɛl vjɛn]	they come/they are coming

- The verb 'venir' takes the preposition 'à' or 'de' when it is followed by the name of a place. It takes 'chez' when it is followed by the name of a person or a personal pronoun.

Examples:

Je viens à Delhi. [ʒə vjɛ̃ a dɛli]	I come to Delhi/ I am coming to Delhi.
Je viens chez Paul. [ʒə vjɛ̃ ʃe pɔl]	I come to Paul's place/ I am coming to Paul's place.
Je viens chez lui. [ʒə vjɛ̃ ʃe lɥi]	I come to his place/ I am coming to his place.
Je viens de Paris. [ʒə vjɛ̃ də pari]	I come from Paris/ I am coming from Paris.
Je viens de chez Paul. [ʒə vjɛ̃ də ʃe pɔl]	I come from Paul's place/ I am coming from Paul's place.
Je viens de chez lui. [ʒə vjɛ̃ də ʃe lɥi]	I come from his place/ I am coming from his place.

Lesson 3

How to talk about somebody — *Comment parler de quelquun*

Mrs. Singh: What is there in your pocket?	Mme. Singh: Qu'est-ce qu'il y a dans ta poche? [kɛskilja dɑ̃ ta pɔʃ]
Mr. Singh: My friend's photograph.	M. Singh: La photo de mon ami. [la fɔtɔ də mɔnami]
Mrs. Singh: Can I see the photograph?	Mme. Singh: Est-ce que je peux voir la photo? [ɛskə ʒə pø vwar la fɔtɔ]
Mr. Singh: Yes. Why not?	M. Singh: Oui. Pourquoi pas? [wi purkwa pa]
Mrs. Singh: Is he European?	Mme. Singh: Est-il european? [ɛtil ørɔpeɛ̃]
M. Singh: No. He is from Canada.	M. Singh: Non. Il vient du Canada. [nɔ̃ il vjɛ̃ dy kanada]

Mrs. Singh: What is his name?	Mme. Singh: Il s'appelle comment? [il sapɛl kəmã]
Mr. Singh: His name is Vincent.	M. Singh: Il s'appelle Vincent. [il sapɛl vɛ̃sã]
Mrs. Singh: What does he do?	Mme. Singh: Qu'est-ce qu'il fait comme métier? [kɛskil fɛ kɔm metie]
Mr. Singh: He is a professor at Sherbrooke University.	M. Singh: Il est professeur à l.université de Sherbrooke. [ilɛ prɔ fɛsœr a lyniversite də ʃɛrbruk]
Mrs. Singh: Is he married?	Mme. Singh: Est-il Marié? [ɛtil marie]
Mr. Singh: No, he is a bachelor.	M. Singh: Non, il est célibataire. [nɔ̃ ilɛ selibatɛr]

Vocabulaire	Vocabulary
la poche (n.f.) [la pɔʃ]	pocket
la photo (n.f.) [la fɔtɔ]	photograph
le métier (n.m.) [lə metje]	profession
l'université (n.f.) [lyniversite]	university
pouvoir (v) [puvwar]	to be able to
voir (v) [vwar]	to see
faire (v) [fɛr]	to do
parler (v) [parle]	to speak

Countries and nationalities

Countries/Les pays	Nationalities/Les nationalités	
L'Inde (India)	indien (m) /indienne (f)	
[lɛ̃d]	[ɛ̃dj ɛ̃]	[ɛ̃djɛn]
La France (France)	français (m) /française (f)	
[la frɑ̃s]	[fr ɑ̃sɛ]	[fr ɑ̃sɛz]
La Suisse (Switzerland)	suisse (m) /suisse (f)	
[la sɥis]	[s ɥis]	[s ɥis]
Le Canada (Canada)	canadien (m) /canadienne (f)	
[ləkanada]	[kanadj ɛ̃]	[kanadjɛn]
L'Angleterre (England)	anglais (m) /anglaise (f)	
[lɑ̃glətɛr]	[ɑ̃glɛ]	[ɑ̃glɛz]
L'Espagne (Spain)	espagnol (m) /espagnole (f)	
[lɛspaɲ]	[ɛspaɲɔl]	[ɛspa ɲɔl]
L'Allemagne (Germany)	allemand (m) /allemande (f)	
[lalmaɲ]	[alm ɑ̃]	[alm ɑ̃d]
La Russie (Russia)	russe(m) /russe (f)	
[la rysi]	[rys]	[rys]
La Chine (China)	chinois (m) /chinoise (f)	
[la ʃin]	[ʃinwa]	[ʃinwaz]

Le Portugal (Portugal)	portugais (m) /portugaise (f)
[lɔ pɔrtygal]	[pɔrtygɛ] [pɔrtygɛz]
L'Italie (Italy)	italien (m) /italienne (f)
[litali]	[italjɛ̃] [italjɛn]
Le Brésil (Brazil)	brésilien (m) /brésilienne (f)
[lə brezil]	[breziljɛ̃] [breziljɛn]
Le Pakistan (Pakistan)	pakistanais (m) /pakistanaise (f)
[lə pakistã]	[pakistanɛ] [pakistanɛz]
Le Japon (Japan)	japonais (m) /japonaise (f)
[lə ʒapɔ̃]	[ʒapɔnɛ] [ʒapɔnɛz]
L'Arabie saudite (Saudi Arabia)	arab (m) /arabe (f)
[larabi saudit]	[arab] [arab]
La Belgique (Belgium)	belge (m) /belge (f)
[la bɛlʒik]	[bɛlʒ] [bɛlʒ]
L'Irlande (Ireland)	irlandais (m) /irlandaise (f)
[lirlãd]	[irlãdɛ] [irlãdɛz]
Les États-Unis (United States) [lezetazyni]	américain (m) /américaine (f)
	[amerikɛ̃] [amerikɛn]
Le Pays-bas (Netherland)	hollandais (m) /hollandaise (f)
[lə pɛj ba]	[ɔlãdɛ] [ɔlãdɛz]

Grammaire *Grammar*

Regular verbs

Regular verbs can be divided into three groups:

1st group verbs: verbs ending in 'er' ('aller' is an exception)

2nd group verbs: verbs ending in 'ir' (finir, choisir etc.)

3rd group verbs: verbs ending in 're', 'ir' (prendre, dépendre, voir etc.)

Le Présent

The **'présent'** is used to describe actions that occur at the moment of speaking.

Example:

Je parle français. I am speaking French.

[ʒə parl frãsɛ]

It also describes repeated actions.

Example:

Je mange du gâteau tous les jours. I eat cake everyday.

[ʒə mãʒ dy gato tu le ʒur]

Conjugation of 1st group verbs in the 'présent'

To conjugate a first group verb in the 'présent' we remove the last 'er' from the infinitive form of the verb and add the following suffixes:

je	**-e**	**nous**	**-ons**
tu	**-es**	**vous**	**-ez**
il	**-e**	**ils**	**-ent**
elle	**-e**	**elles**	**-ent**

Examples:

parler

je parle [ʒə parl]	I speak/I am speaking
tu parles [ty parl]	you speak/you are speaking
il parle [il parl]	he speaks/he is speaking
elle parle [ɛl parl]	she speaks/she is speaking
nous parlons [nu parlʒ]	we speak/we are speaking
vous parlez [vu parle]	you speak/you are speaking
ils parlent [il parl]	they speak/they are speaking
elles parlent [ɛl parl]	they speak/they are speaking

- The verb 'parler' takes the preposition 'à' or 'de' depending upon the context.

Examples:

Je parle à Paul. [ʒə parl a pɔl]	I speak to Paul/ I am Speaking to Paul.
Je parle de Paul. [ʒə parl dəpɔl]	I speak about Paul/ I am speaking about Paul.
Je parle de Paris. [ʒə parl də pari]	I speak about Paris/ I am speaking about Paris.

habiter

j'habite [ʒabit]	I live/I am living
tu habites [ty abit]	you live/you are living
il habite [ilabit]	he lives/he is living
elle habite [ɛlabit]	she lives/she is living
nous habitons [nuzabitɔ̃]	we live/we are living
vous habitez [vuzabite]	you live/you are living
ils habitent [ilzabit]	they live/they are living
elles habitent [ɛlzabit]	they live /they are living

- The verb 'habiter' takes the preposition 'à', 'dans' or 'chez' depending upon the context.

Examples:

J'habite à Delhi. [ʒabita dɛli]	I live in Delhi/ I am living in Delhi.
J'habite dans cette maison. [ʒabit dɑ̃ sɛt mɛzɔ̃]	I live in this house/ I am living in this house.
J'habite chez Paul. [ʒabit ʃe pɔl]	I live in Paul's house/ I am living in Paul's house.

Other verbs

pouvoir

('pouvoir' is an irregular verb)

je peux [ʒə pø]	I can
tu peux [ty pø]	you can
il peut [il pø]	he can
elle peut [ɛl pø]	she can
nous pouvons [nu puvɔ̃]	we can
vous Pouvez [vu puve]	you can
ils peuvent [il pœv]	they can
elles peuvent [ɛl pœv]	they can

❖ The verb 'pouvoir' is always followed by the infinitive form of a verb.

Examples:

Je peux parler. [ʒə pø parle]	I can speak.
Je peux aller. [ʒə pø ale]	I can go.
Je peux voir. [ʒə pø vwar]	I can see.
Je peux parler français. [ʒə pø parle frɑ̃se]	I can speak French.
Je peux aller à Paris. [ʒə pø ale a pari]	I can go to Paris.
Je peux voir la photo. [ʒə pø vwar la fɔtɔ]	I can see the photograph.

voir

('voir' is an irregular verb)

je vois [ʒə vwa]	I see
tu vois [ty vwa]	you see
il voit [il vwa]	he sees
elle voit [ɛl vwa]	she sees
nous voyons [nu vwajɔ̃]	we see

vous voyez — you see
[vu vwaje]
ils voient — they see
[il vwa]
elles voient — they see
[ɛl vwa]

❖ The verb 'voir' does not take any preposition.

Examples:

Je vois une photo. — I see a photograph.
[ʒə vwa yn fɔtɔ]

Je vois Paul. — I see Paul.
[ʒə vwa pɔl]

Je vois mon ami. — I see my friend.
[ʒə vwa mɔnami]

faire

('faire' is an irregular verb)

je fais — I do/I am doing
[ʒ fɛ]
tu fais — you do/you are doing
[ty fɛ]
il fait — he does/he is doing
[il fɛ]
elle fait — she does/she is doing
[ɛl fɛ]
nous faisons — we do/we are doing
[nu fəzã]

vous faites	you do/you are doing
[vu fɛt]	
ils font	they do/they are doing
[il fɔ̃]	
elles font	they do/they are doing
[ɛl fɔ̃]	

❖ *The verb 'faire' does not take any preposition.*

Examples:

Je fais mon devoir.	I do my work/
[ʒə fɛ mɔ̃ dəvwar]	I am doing my work.
Je fais des exercices.	I do the exercises/
[ʒə fɛ dezɛgzɛrsis]	I am doing the exercises.

Lesson 4

How to talk about your family — Comment parler de votre famille

Mr. Vincent: Singh, do you stay with your family in Delhi?	M. Vincent: Singh, tu habites avec ta famille à Delhi? [siŋ ty abit avɛk ta famij a dɛli]
Mr. Singh: Yes, I stay with my wife and my daughter.	M. Singh: Oui. J'habite avec ma femme et ma fille. [wi ʒabit avɛk ma fam e ma fij]
Mr. Vincent: What does your wife do?	M. Vincent: Qu'est-ce que ta femme fait dans la vie? [kɛskə ta fam fɛ dɑ̃ la vi]
Mr. Singh: She is a house wife.	M. Singh: Elle est femme au foyer. [ɛlɛ fam o fwaje]
Mr. Vincent: And your daughter?	M. Vincent: Et ta fille? [e ta fij]
Mr. Singh: She works in a multinational company.	M. Singh: Elle travaille dans une société mutinationale. [ɛl travaj dɑ̃zyn sɔsjete myltinasjɔnal]
Mr. Vincent: I would like to meet them sometime.	M. Vincent: Je voudrais les rencontrer un de ces jours. [ʒə vudrɛ le rɑ̃kɔ̃trœ̃də se ʒur]

Vocabulaire	*Vocabulary*
la vie (n.f.) [la vi]	life
la femme au foyer (n.f.) [la fam o fwaje]	housewife
la société (n.f.) [la sɔsjete]	company/society
la société multinationale (n.f.) [la sɔsjete myltinasjɔnal]	multinational company
travailler (v) [travaje]	to work
rencontrer (v) [rãkɔ̃tre]	to meet

La famille

les grands-parents [le grã parã]	grandparents
le grand-père [lə grã pɛr]	grandfather
la grand-mère [la grã mɛr]	grandmother

les parents [le parã]	parents
le père [lə pɛr]	father
la mère [la mɛr]	mother
le frère [lə frɛr]	brother
la sœur [la sœr]	sister
l'oncle [lɔ̃kl]	uncle
la tante [la tɔ̃t]	aunt
le cousin [lə kuzɛ̃]	cousin
la cousine [la kuzin]	cousin
la femme [la fam]	wife
les enfants [le zãfã]	children
le fils [lə fis]	son

la fille [la fij]	daughter
les petits-enfants [le pəti zãfã]	grandchildren
le petit-fils [lə pəti fis]	grandson
La petite-fille [la pətit fij]	granddaughter
les beaux-parents [le bo parã]	in laws
le beau-père [lə bo pɛr]	father-in-law
la belle-mère [la bɛl mɛr]	mother-in-law
le beau-frère [lə bo frɛr]	brother-in-law
la belle-sœur [la bɛl sœr]	sister-in-law

Grammaire | *Grammar*

Possessive adjectives/Les adjectifs possessifs

Possessive Adjectives	Poss. adj. used with mas. sing. nouns/ fem. sing. nouns starting with a vowel	Poss. adj. used with fem. sing nouns	Poss. adj. used with plural nouns
my	Mon [mɔ̃]	ma [ma]	mes [me]
your	ton [tɔ̃]	ta [ta]	tes [te]
his/her	son [sɔ̃]	sa [sa]	ses [se]
our	notre [nɔtr]	notre [nɔtr]	nos [no]
your	votre [vɔtr]	votre [vɔtr]	vos [vo]
their	leur [lœr]	leur [lœr]	leurs [lœr]

Examples:
Mon/ton/son/notre/votre/leur frère
My/your/his/her/our/your/their brother

Ma/ta/sa/notre/votre/leur soeur
My/your/his/her/our/your/their sister

Mon/ton/son/notre/votre/leur amie
My/your/his/her/our/your/their friend

Mes/tes/ses/nos/vos/leurs frères
My/your/his/her/our/your/their brothers

Mes/tes/ses/nos/vos/leurs soeurs
My/your/his/her/our/your/their sisters

Mes/tes/ses/nos/vos/leurs amies
My/your/his/her/our/your/their friends

Prepositions/Les prépositions

sur (on)
[syr]
Le chat est sur la table. The cat is on the table.
[lə ʃa ɛ syr la tabl]

sous (under)
[su]
Le chat est sous la table. The cat is under the table.
[lə ʃa ɛ su la tabl]

devant (in front of)
[də vã]
Le chat est devant la table. The cat is in front of the table.
[lə ʃa ɛ dəvã la tabl]

à côté de (beside)
[a kote də]
Le chat est à côté de la table. The cat is beside the table.
[lə ʃa ɛta kote də la tabl]

derrière (behind)

[dɛrjɛr]

Le chat est derrière la table. The cat is behind the table.

[lə ʃa ɛ dɛrjɛr la tabl]

à droite de (on the right side of)

[a drwat də]

Le chat est à droite de la table. The cat is on the right side of the table.

[lə ʃa ɛ ta drwatəd la tabl]

à gauche de (on the left side of)

[a goʃ də]

Le chat est à gauche de la table. The cat is on the left side of the table.

[ləʃa ɛta goʃ dəla tabl]

près de (near)

[prɛ də]

Le chat est près de la table. The cat is near the table.

[lə ʃa ɛ prɛ dəla tabl]

loin de (far from)

[lwɛ̃ də]

Le chat est loin de la table. The cat is far from the table.

[ləʃa ɛ lwɛ̃də la tabl]

dans (in/inside)

[dɑ̃]

La table est dans la salle. The table is in the hall.

[la tabl ɛ dɑ̃ la sal]

avec (with)

[avɛk]

Il joue avec son ami. He plays with his friend.

[il ʒu avɛk sɔ̃nami]

sans (without)

[sɑ̃]

Il joue sans son ami. He plays without his friend.

[il ʒu sɑ̃sɔ̃nami]

Object pronouns/Les pronoms objets

An object pronoun is used to replace a noun acting as an object in a sentence. There are two types of object pronouns.

Direct object pronouns/Les pronoms objets directs

When the pronoun replaces a direct object, it is called direct object pronoun (pronom objet direct)

	Singular	**Plural**
1st person	me (me) [mə]	nous (us) [nu]
2nd person	te (you) [t ə]	vous (you) [vu]
3rd person	le (mas.) (him/it) [lə]	les (them) [le]
	la (fem.) [la]	

Examples:

Je regarde **la photo.** — I look at the photograph.
[ʒə rəgard la fɔtɔ]

Je **la** regarde. — I look at it.
[ʒə la rəgard]

❖ In the above sentence, the pronoun 'la' replaces 'la photo' which is a direct object. In French, direct and indirect object pronouns are always placed before the verb.

Je regarde **les photos.** — I look at the photographs.
[ʒə rəgard le fɔtɔ]

Je <u>**les**</u> regarde. — I look at them.
[ʒ le rəgard]

Indirect object pronouns/Les pronoms objets indirects

When the pronoun replaces an indirect object, it is called indirect object pronoun (pronom objet indirect).

	Singular	Plural
1st person	me (me) [mə]	nous (us) [nu]
2nd person	te (you) [tə]	vous (you) [vu]
3rd person	lui (him/ her) [lɥi]	leur (them) [lœr]

Examples:

Je parle à **Paul.** — I speak to Paul.
[ʒə parl a pɔl]

Je **lui** parle. — I speak to him.
[ʒə lɥi parl]

❖ In the above sentence, the pronoun 'lui' replaces 'Paul' which is an indirect object.

Je montre **la photo à Paul.** — I show the photograph to Paul.
[ʒə mɔ̃tr la fɔtɔ a pɔl]

Je la lui montre. — I show it to him.
[ʒə la lɥi mɔ̃ tr]

Lesson 5

How to tell / ask for the time | *Comment demander / dire l'heure*

Mrs. Singh: What is the time?

Mme. Singh: Quelle heure est-il?
[kɛlœr ɛtil]

Mr. Singh: It's 8 O'clock.

M. Singh: Il est huit heures.
[ilɛ ɥitœr]

Mrs. Singh: What time do you have to leave?

Mme. Singh: A quelle heure dois-tu partir?
[a kɛlœr dwa ty partir]

Mr. Singh: At 9.30.

M. Singh: A 9 h 30.
[a nœvœr trɑ̃t]

Mrs. Singh: Hurry up then.

Mme. Singh: Alors, dépêche-toi.
[alɔr depɛʃtwa]

It's 1 a.m.	Il est une heure. [ilɛ ynœr]
It's 2 a.m.	Il est deux heures. [ilɛ døzœr]
It's 3 a.m.	Il est trois heures. [ilɛ trwazœr]
It's 8 a.m.	Il est huit heures. [ilɛ ɥitœr]
It's 11 a.m.	Il est onze heures. [ilɛ ɔ̃zœr]
It's 12 p.m.	Il est midi. [ilɛ midi]
It's 1 p.m.	Il est treize heures/ [ilɛ trɛzœr] Il est une heure de l'après-midi. [ilɛ ynœr də laprɛ midi]
It's 2 p.m.	Il est quatorze heures/ [ilɛ katərzœr] Il est deux heures de l'après-midi. [ilɛ døzœr də laprɛ midi]
It's 10 p.m.	Il est vingt-deux heures/ [ilɛ vɛ̃tdøzœr] Il est dix heures du soir. [ilɛ dizœr dy swar]
It's 12 a.m.	Il est zéro heure/ Il est minuit. [ilɛ zero œr] [ilɛ minɥi]

It's 9.10 a.m.	Il est neuf heures dix. [ilɛ nœvœr dis]
It's 9.15 a.m.	Il est neuf heures quinze/ [ilɛ nœvœr kɛ̃z] Il est neuf heure et quart. [ilɛ nœvœre kar]
It's 9.20 a.m.	Il est neuf heures vingt. [ilɛ nœvœr vɛ̃]
It's 9.30 a.m.	Il est neuf heures trente/ [ilɛ nœvœr trɑ̃t] Il est neuf heures et demie. [ilɛ nœvœre dəmi]
It's 9.45 a.m.	Il est neuf heures quarante-cinq/ [ilɛ nœvœr karɑ̃t sɛ̃k] Il est dix heures moins le quart. [ilɛ dizœr mwɛ̃ lə kar]
It's 9.50 a.m.	Il est neuf heures cinquante/ [ilɛ nœvœr sɛ̃kɑ̃t] Il est dix heures moins dix. [ilɛ dizœr mwɛ̃ dis]

Vocabulaire	Vocabulary
l'heure (n.f.) [lœr]	time/hour
devoir (v) [dəvwar]	should/must/have to
partir (v) [partir]	to leave
se dépêcher (v) [sə depɛʃe]	to hurry

Reflexive verbs/Les verbes pronominaux

Verbs having 'se' before them are called reflexive verbs. They are conjugated with reflexive pronouns: me ,te, se, nous, vous, se.

se lever (to get up)

je me lève [ʒəməlɛv]	I get up
tu te lèves [ty təlɛv]	you get up
il se lève [il sə lɛv]	he gets up
elle se lève [ɛl sə lɛv]	she gets up
nous nous levons [nu nu ləvɔ̃]	we get up
vous vous levez [vu vu ləve]	you get up
ils se lèvent [il səlɛv]	they get up
elles se lèvent [ɛl sə lɛv]	they get up

s'appeler

je m'appelle [ʒə mapɛl]	my name is../I am called..

tu t'appelles [ty tapɛl]	your name is../you are called..
il s'appelle [il sapɛl]	his name is../he is called..
elle s'appelle [ɛl sapɛl]	her name is../she is called..
nous nous appelons [nu nuzaplɔ̃]	our names are../we are called..
vous vous appelez [vu vuzaple]	your names are../you are called..
ils s'appellent [il sapɛl]	their names are../they are called..
elles s'appellent [ɛl sapɛl]	their names are../they are called..

Examples:

Je m'appelle Paul. [ʒə mapɛl pɔl]	My name is Paul.
Tu t'appelles Thierry. [ty tapɛl tjɛri]	Your name is Thierry.
Il s'appelle Jean. [il sapɛl ʒã]	His name is Jean.

Other Verbs

devoir

('devoir' is an irregular verb)

je dois [ʒə dwa]	I should/I must/I have to

tu dois [ty dwa]	you should/you must/ you have to
il doit [il dwa]	he should/he must/ he has to
elle doit [ɛl dwa]	she should/she must/ she has to
nous devons [nu dəvɔ̃]	we should/we must/ we have to
vous devez [vu dəve]	you should/you must/you have to
ils doivent [il dwav]	they should/they must/ they have to
elles doivent [ɛl dwav]	they should/they must/ they have to

❖ The verb 'devoir' is always followed by the infinitive form of a verb.

Examples:

Je dois parler à mon ami. [ʒə dwa parle a mɔ̃nami]	I should speak to my friend / I have to speak to my friend.
Je dois aller à paris. [ʒə dwa ale a pari]	I should go to Paris/ I have to go to Paris.
Je dois travailler. [ʒə dwa travaje]	I should work/I have to work.

partir

je pars [ʒə par]	I leave/I am leaving
tu pars [ty par]	you leave/you are leaving
il part [il par]	he leaves/he is leaving
elle part [ɛl par]	she leaves/she is leaving
nous partons [nu partɔ̃]	we leave/we are leaving
vous partez [vu parte]	you leave/you are leaving
ils partent [il part]	they leave/they are leaving
elles partent [ɛl part]	they leave/they are leaving

- The verb 'partir' takes the preposition 'à' or 'de' depending upon the context.

Examples:

Je pars à Paris. [ʒə par a pari]	I leave for Paris/ I am leaving for Paris.
Je pars de Delhi. [ʒə par də deli]	I leave Delhi/I am leaving Delhi.

Lesson 6

How to talk about your daily routine — *Comment parler de votre journée*

Sylvie: Paul, you always come to the office on time. What time do you wake up?

Sylvie: Paul, tu viens toujours au bureau à l'heure. Tu te réveilles à quelle heure ?
[pɔl ty vjɛ̃ tuʒur o byro a lœr] [ty tə revɛj a kɛlœr]

Paul: I always wake up at 7 O'clock. Then I take a bath and get ready in 20 minutes. I take my breakfast at 8 O'clock and leave for the office at 8.30.

Paul: Je me réveille toujours à 7h. Puis je prends mon bain et je m'habille en 20 minutes. Je prends le petit déjeuner à 8h et je pars au bureau à 8h 30.
[ʒə mə revɛj tuʒur a sɛtœr] [pɥi ʒə prɑ̃ mɔ̃ bɛ̃ e ʒə mabij ɑ̃ vɛ̃ minyt] [ʒə prɑ̃ lə pəti dejœne a ɥitœr e ʒə par o byro a ɥitœr trɑ̃t]

Sylvie: You don't read news papers?

Sylvie: Tu ne lis pas de journal ?
[ty nə li pa də ʒurnal]

Paul: Yes. I return home at 5 p.m. I take a shower and then I read news papers.	Paul : Si. Je rentre chez moi à 17 h. Je prends une douche. Puis je lis des journaux. [si ʒə rãtr ʃe mwa a disɛtoer ʒə prã yn duʃ pɥi ʒə li de ʒurno]
Sylvie: What time do you have your dinner?	Sylvie: A quelle heure tu prends le dîner ? [a kɛlœr ty pr ãl ədine]
Paul: I have my dinner at 8 O' clock.	Paul: Je prends le dîner à 20h. [ʒə pr ã lə dine a vɛ̃toer]
Sylvie: You go to bed early?	Sylvie: Tu te couche tôt ? [ty tə kuʃ to]
Paul: No. I study till 11 O. clock and sleep at 11.30.	Paul: Non, j'étudie jusqu'à 23 h et je dors à 23 h 30. [nɔ̃ ʒetydi ʒyska vɛ̃t trwazœr e ʒə dor a vɛ̃t trwazœr trãt]

Vocabulaire	Vocabulary
le bureau (n.m.) [lə byro]	office
le bain (n.m.) [lə bɛ̃]	bath
le petit déjeuner (n.m.) [lə pəti deʒœne]	breakfast
le journal (n.m.) [lə ʒurnal]	newspaper
la douche (n.f.) [la duʃ]	shower
le dîner (n.m.) [lə dine]	dinner
toujours (adv.) [tuʒur]	always
puis (adv.) [pɥi]	then
tôt (adv.) [to]	early
jusque (prep.) [ʒyskə]	till

se réveiller (v) [sə revεje]	to wake up
prendre (v) [prãdr]	to take
s'habiller (v) [sabije]	to dress up
lire (v) [lir]	to read
rentrer (v) [rãtre]	to return
se coucher (v) [sə kuʃe]	to go to bed
étudier (v) [etydje]	to study
dormir (v) [dɔrmir]	to sleep

Plural of nouns and adjectives

Generally, we add an 's' to a noun or an adjective to get its plural form.

le jour (n)	les jours
[lə ʒur]	[le ʒur]
la nuit (n)	les nuits
[la nɥi]	[le n ɥi]
l'orange (n)	les oranges
[lɔrãʒ]	[lez ɔr ãʒ]
grand (adj.)	grands
[grã]	[gr ã]
petit (adj.)	petits
[pəti]	[pəti]

❖ *If we want to get the plural form of a noun ending in 'eau' or 'eu', we add an 'x' to it.*

le manteau (n)	les manteaux
[lə mã to]	[le m ãto]
le neveu (n)	les neveux
[lə nəvø]	[le nəvø]

❖ *If a noun or an adjective is ending in 'al', we remove 'al' and put 'aux' to get its plural form.*

l'hôpital (n)	les hôpitaux
[lɔpital]	[lezəpito]
national (adj.)	nationaux
[nasjɔnal]	[nasj ɔno]

❖ *A noun or an adjective ending in 's', 'x' or 'z' does not change in plural.*

le bras (n)	les bras
[lə bra]	[le bra]
le nez (n)	les nez
[lə ne]	[le ne]
la croix (n)	les croix
[la krwa]	[le krwa]
chaleureux (adj.)	chaleureux
[ʃalœrø]	[ʃalœrø]
bas (adj.)	bas
[ba]	[ba]

Verbs

se réveiller

je me réveille [ʒə mə revɛj]	I wake up/I am waking up
tu te réveilles [ty tə revɛj]	you wake up/you are waking up
il se réveille [il sə revɛj]	he wakes up/he is waking up
elle se réveille [ɛl sə revɛj]	she wakes up/she is waking up
nous nous réveillons [nu nu revɛjɔ̃]	we wake up/we are waking up
vous vous réveillez [vu vu revɛje]	you wake up/you are waking up

ils se réveillent [il sə revɛj]	they wake up/ they are waking up
elles se réveillent [ɛl sə revɛj]	they wake up/ they are waking up

Example:

Je me réveille tôt. [ʒə mə revɛj to]	I wake up early.

prendre

je prends [ʒə pr ã]	I take/I am taking
tu prends [ty pr ã]	you take/you are taking
il prend [il pr ã]	he takes/he is taking
elle prend [ɛl prã]	she takes/she is taking
nous prenons [nu prənɔ̃]	we take/we are taking
vous prenez [vu prəne]	you take/you are taking
ils prennent [il prɛn]	they take/they are taking
elles prennent [ɛl prɛn]	they take/they are taking

❖ *The verb 'prendre' does not take any preposition.*

Example:

Je prends une douche.	I take/I am taking a shower.
[ʒə prã yn du]	
Je prends le petit déjeuner.	I take/I am taking breakfast.
[ʒə prã lə pəti deʒœne]	

s'habiller

je m'habille	I dress up/I am
[ʒə mabij]	dressing up
tu t'habilles	you dress up/you are
[ty tabij]	dressing up
il s'habille	he dresses up/he is
[il sabij]	dressing up
elle s'habille	she dresses up/she is
[ɛl sabij]	dressing up
nous nous habillons	we dress up/we are
[nu nu zabijɔ̃]	dressing up
vous vous habillez	you dress up/you are
[vu vu zabije]	dressing up
ils s'habillent	they dress up/they are
[il sabij]	dressing up
elles s'habillent	they dress up/they are
[ɛl sabij]	dressing up

Example:

Je m'habille à 7 heures.	I dress up at 7 O'clock.
[ʒə mabij a sɛtoer]	

lire

je lis	I read/I am reading
[ʒə li]	
tu lis	you read/you are reading
[ty li]	
il lit	he reads/he is reading
[il li]	
elle lit	she reads/she is reading
[ɛl li]	
nous lisons	we read/we are reading
[nu liz ɔ̃]	
vous lisez	you read/you are reading
[vu lize]	
ils lisent	they read/they are reading
[il liz]	
elles lisent	they read/they are reading
[ɛl liz]	

❖ *The verb 'lire' does not take any preposition.*

Example:

Je lis un journal. — I am reading a newspaper.

[ʒə liœ̃ ʒurnal]

rentrer

je rentre	I return/I am returning
[ʒə rã tr]	
tu rentres	you return/you are returning
[ty rã tr]	

il rentre [il rã tr]	he returns/he is returning
elle rentre [ɛl rã tr]	she returns/she is returning
nous rentrons [nu rã tr ɔ̃]	we return/we are returning
vous rentrez [vu rã tre]	you return/you are returning
ils rentrent [il rã tr]	they return/they are returning
elles rentrent [ɛl rã tr]	they return/they are returning

❖ *The verb 'rentrer' takes the preposition 'à' or 'de' depending upon the context.*

Examples:

Je rentre à Delhi. [ʒə rã tr a dɛli]	I return/I am returning to Delhi.
Je rentre de Paris. [ʒə rã tr də pari]	I return/I am returning from Paris.

se coucher

je me couche [ʒə mə kuʃ]	I go to bed/I am going to bed
tu te couches [ty tə kuʃ]	you go to bed/you are going to bed
il se couche [il sə kuʃ]	he goes to bed/he is going to bed

elle se couche — she goes to bed/she is going to bed
[ɛl sə kuʃ]
nous nous couchons — we go to bed/we are going to bed
[nu nu kuʃɔ̃]
vous vous couchez — you go to bed/you are going to bed
[vu vu kuʃe]
ils se couchent — they go to bed/they are going to bed
[il sə kuʃ]
elles se couchent — they go to bed/they are going to bed
[ɛl sə kuʃ]

étudier

j'étudie — I study/I am studying
[ʒətydi]
tu étudies — you study/you are studying
[ty etydi]
il étudie — he studies/he is studying
[il etydi]
elle étudie — she studies/she is studying
[ɛl etydi]
nous étudions — we study/we are studying
[nuzetydj ɔ̃]
vous étudiez — you study/you are studying
[vuzetydje]
ils étudient — they study/they are studying
[il zetydi]
elles étudient — they study/they are studying
[ɛl zetydi]

dormir

('dormir' is an irregular verb)

je dors [ʒə dɔr]	I sleep/I am sleeping
tu dors [ty dɔr]	you sleep/you are sleeping
il dort [il dɔr]	he sleeps/he is sleeping
elle dort [ɛl dɔr]	she sleeps/she is sleeping
nous dormons [nu dɔrmɔ̃]	we sleep/we are sleeping
vous dormez [vu dɔrme]	you sleep/you are sleeping
ils dorment [il dɔrm]	they sleep/they are sleeping
elles dorment [ɛl dɔrm]	they sleep/they are sleeping

Lesson 7

Leisure activities — *Les rencontres*

Paul: Hi Thierry. What are you doing?	Paul: Salut , Thierry. Qu'est-ce que tu fais ? [saly tjɛri kɛskə ty fɛ]
Thierry: I am doing my homework.	Thierry: Je fais mes devoirs à la maison. [ʒə fɛ me dəvwar a la mɛzɔ̃]
Paul: You study on week-ends?	Paul: Tu étudies le week-end ? [ty etydi lə wikɛ̃d]
Thierry: Yes. You do not study on week-ends?	Thierry: Oui. Tu n'études pas le week-end. [wi ty netydi pa lə wikɛ̃d]
Paul: No. I never work on week-ends.	Paul: Non. Je ne travaille jamais le week-end. [nɔ̃ ʒə nə travaj ʒame lə wikɛ̃d]

Thierry: Then what do you do?	Thierry: Alors, qu'est-ce que tu fais ? [alɔr kɛskə ty fɛ]
Paul: I watch T.V., play cricket and listen to music. I enjoy a lot on week-ends.	Paul: Je regarde la télévision, joue au cricket et écoute la musique. Je m'amuse beaucoup pendant le week-end. [ʒə regard la televizjɔ̃ ʒu o krikete ekute la myzik] [ʒə mamyz boku pɑ̃dɑ̃ lə wikɛnd]

Vocabulaire	Vocabulary
le devoir à la maison (n.m.) [lə dəvwar a la mɛzɔ̃]	homework
la télévision (n.f.) [la televizjɔ̃]	television
le cricket (n.m.) [lə kriket]	cricket
la musique (n.f.) [la myzik]	music
le week-end (n.m.) [lə wikənd]	week-end
travailler (v) [travaje]	to work
regarder (v) [rəgarde]	to look at/to watch
jouer (v) [ʒwe]	to play
écouter (v) [ekute]	to listen
s'amuser (v) [samyze]	to enjoy oneself

Grammaire / *Grammar*

Negation

To change a sentence to negative, we put 'ne' before the verb and 'pas' after the verb.

Examples:

Je parle français. [ʒə parl frãsɛ]	I speak French.
Je ne parle pas français. [ʒə nə parl pa frãsɛ]	I do not speak French.

- *If you want to say 'I never speak French' put 'ne' before the verb and 'jamais' after the verb.*

Example:

Je ne parle jamais français. [ʒə nə parl ʒame frãsɛ]	I never speak French.

- *If you want to say 'I do not speak French any more' put 'ne' before the verb and 'plus' after the verb.*

Example:

Je ne parle plus français. [ʒə nə parl ply frãsɛ]	I do not speak French any more.

Interrogative sentences/Les phrases interrogatives-I

We can make an interrogative sentence by simply putting a question mark after an affirmative sentence while writing and using a rising intonation while speaking.

Example:

Tu parles français? Do you speak French?

[ty parl frãsɛ]

❖ *An interrogative sentence can also be made by using 'est-ce-que' before an affirmative sentence.*

Example:

Est-ce-que tu parles français ? Do you speak French?

[ɛskə ty parl frãsɛ]

❖ *In a formal situation we generally make an interrogative sentence by putting the verb before the subject.*

Example:

Parles-tu français? Do you speak French?

[parl ty frãsɛ]

Verbs

travailler

je travaille [ʒə travaj]	I work/I am working
tu travailles [ty travaj]	you work/you are working
il travaille [il travaj]	he works/he is working
elle travaille [ɛl travaj]	she works/she is working
nous travaillons	we work/we are working

[nu travaj]	
vous travaillez [vu travaje]	you work/you are working
ils travaillent [il travaj]	they work/they are working
elles travaillent [ɛl travaj]	they work/they are working

Example:

Je travaille dûr. [ʒə travaj dyr]	I work/I am working hard.

regarder

je regarde [r gard]	I look at../I am looking at.. I watch../I am watching..
tu regardes [ty r gard]	you look at../you are looking at.. you watch../you are watching..
il regarde [il r gard]	he looks at../he is looking at.. he watches../he is watching..
elle regarde [ɛl r gard]	she looks at../she is looking at.. she watches../she is watching..
nous regardons [nu r gard]	we look at../we are looking at.. we watch../we are watching..
vous regardez [vu r garde]	you look at../you are looking at.. you watch../you are watching..
ils regardent	they look at../they are looking at..

[il r gard]	they watch../they are watching..
elles regardent	they look at/they are looking at
[ɛl r gard]	they watch/they are watching

❖ *The verb „ regarder. does not take any preposition*

Example:

Je regarde la télé.	I watch T.V./I am watching T.V.
[ʒ r gard la tele]	

jouer

je joue	I play/I am playing
[ʒ ʒu]	
tu joues	you play/you are playing
[ty ʒu]	
il joue	he plays/he is playing
[il ʒu]	
elle joue	she plays/she is playing
[ɛl ʒu]	
nous jouons	we play/we are playing
[nu ʒuɔ̃]	
vous jouez	you play/you are playing
[vu ʒwe]	
ils jouent	they play/they are playing
[il ʒu]	
elles jouent	they play/they are playing
[ɛl ʒu]	

❖ *The verb 'jouer' takes 'à' when it is followed by the name of a game. It takes 'de' when it is followed by the name of a musical instrument.*

Examples:

Je joue au cricket. [ʒə ʒu o kriket]	I play cricket/I am playing cricket.
Je joue de la guitare. [ʒə ʒu də la gitar]	I play guitar/ I am playing guitar.

écouter

j'écoute [ʒekut]	I listen/I am listening
tu écoutes [ty ekut]	you listen/you are listening
il écoute [il ekut]	he listens/he is listening
elle écoute [ɛl ekut]	she listens/she is listening
nous écoutons [nuzekutɔ̃]	we listen/we are listening
vous écoutez [vuzekute]	you listen/you are listening
ils écoutent [ilzekut]	they listen/they are listening
elles écoutent [ɛlzekut]	they listen/they are listening

❖ *The verb 'écouter' does not take any preposition.*

Example:

J'écoute la radio. I listen to the radio/

[ʒekut la radjo]	I am listening to the radio.

s'amuser

je m'amuse [ʒə mamyz]	I enjoy myself/I am enjoying myself
tu t'amuses [ty tamyz]	you enjoy yourself/you are enjoying yourself
il s'amuse [il samyz]	he enjoys himself/he is enjoying himself
elle s'amuse [ɛl samyz]	she enjoys herself/she is enjoying herself
nous nous amusons [nu nuzamyzɔ̃]	we enjoy ourselves/we are enjoying ourselves
vous vous amusez [vu vuzamyze]	you enjoy yourself/you are enjoying yourself
ils s'amusent [il samyz]	they enjoy themselves/they are enjoying themselves
elles s'amusent [ɛl samyz]	they enjoy themselves/they are enjoying themselves

Example:

Je m'amuse beaucoup. I enjoy myself a lot.

Lesson 8

Weather — *Le temps*

Samia: Hi Sophie.	Samia: Salut, Sophie. [saly sofi]
Sophie: Hi Samia.	Sophie: Salut, Samia. [saly samja]
Samia: How is the weather like in France?	Samia: Quel temps fait-il en France ? [kɛl tã fɛtil ã frãs]
Sophie: In France , it is cold.	Sophie: Il fait froid en France. [il fɛ frwa ã frãs]
Samia: Is it always cold in France?	Samia: Il fait toujours froid en France ? [il fɛ tuʒur frwa ã frãs]
Sophie: No from January till March, It's cold. But from July till September, it's hot.	Sophie: Non, du janvier jusqu au mars, il fait froid. Mais du juillet jusqu'au septembre, il fait chaud.

	[nɔ̃ dy ʒɑ̃vje ʒysko mars il fɛ frwa mɛ dy ʒɥije ʒysko sɛptɑ̃br il fɛ ʃo]
Samia: It doesn't rain in France?	Samia: Il ne pleut pas en France ? [il nə plø pazɑ̃ frɑ̃s]
Sophie: Yes, from October till December, it rains.	Sophie: Si, de l'octobre jusqu.au décembre, il pleut. [si də lɔkɔtbr ʒysko desɑ̃br il plø]
Samia: I want to come to France in April. What is the weather like in April?	Samia: Je veux venir en France en avril. Quel temps fait-il en avril ? [ʒə vø vənir ɑ̃ frɑ̃s ɑ̃navril kɛl tɑ̃ fɛtil ɑ̃navril]
Sophie: In April, It's pleasant.	Sophie: En avril, il fait beau. [ɑ̃navril il fɛ bo]

Vocabulaire	*Vocabulary*
le temps (n.m.)	weather
[lə tã]	
froid (adj.)	cold
[frwa]	
chaud(adj.)	hot ,
[ʃo]	
beau (adj.)	pleasant/fine/
[bo]	beautiful/handsome
pleuvoir (v)	to rain
[pløvwar]	

Les saisons	**Seasons**
l'automne (n.m.)	Autumn
[lotɔn]	
le printemps(n.m.)	Spring
[lə prɛ̃tã]	
l'été (n.m.)	Summer
[lete]	
l'hiver (n.m.)	Winter
[livɛr]	

Les jours de la semaine	**Days of the week**
lundi	Monday
[lœ̃di]	
mardi	Tuesday
[mardi]	
mercredi	Wednesday
[mɛrkrədi]	

jeudi — Thursday
[ʒødi]
vendredi — Friday
[vãdrədi]
samedi — Saturday
[samdi]
Dimanche — Sunday
[dimãʃ]

Les mois de l'anneé	**Months of the year**
janvier [ʒãvje]	January
février [fevrie]	February
mars [mars]	March
avril [avril]	April
mai [mɛ]	May
juin [ʒɥɛ̃]	June
juillet [ʒɥijɛ]	July
août [ut]	August
septembre [sɛptãbr]	September
octobre [ɔktɔbr]	October
novembre [nɔvãbr]	November
décembre [desãbr]	December

Grammaire *Grammar*

Interrogative sentences-II

A question can also be asked' by using interrogative adjectives (quel, quels, quelle, quelles) or interrogative pronouns (où, comment, quand etc.)

- Quel jour est-ce aujourd'hui ?
  [kɛl ʒur ɛ sə oʒurdɥi]
  What is the day today?
- Quel temps fait-il aujourd'hui ?
  [kɛl tã fɛtil oʒurdɥi]
  What is the weather like today?
- Quelle chanson chante-t-il ?
  [kɛl ʃãsõ ʃãtil]
  What song does he sing?
- Qu.est-ce que tu fais ?
  [kɛskə ty fɛ]
  What do you do/what are you doing?
- Que fais-tu?
  [kə fɛ ty]
  What do you do/what are you doing?
- Où habites-tu?
  [u abit ty]
  Where do you live?
- Quand vient-il chez toi ?
  [kã vjɛ̃ til ʃe twa]
  When does he come to your place?
- Comment vient-il chez toi ?
  [kəmã vjɛ̃ til ʃe twa]
  How does he come to your place?
- Pourquoi vient-il chez toi ?
  [purkwa vjɛ̃ til ʃe twa]
  Why does he come to your place?

Contracted articles/ Articles contractés

- *When 'à' is followed by 'le', it becomes 'au'.*

Example:

Je vais (à le) Japon.
Je vais **au** Japon. I am going to Japan.
[ʒə ve o ʒapɔ̃]

- *When 'à' is followed by 'les' it becomes 'aux'.*

Example:

Je vais (à les) États-Unis.
Je vais **aux** États-Unis. I am going to United States.
[ʒə ve ozetazyni]

- *When 'à' is followed by 'la', it remains 'à la'. But it becomes 'en' when 'la' is followed by the name of a country.*

Examples:

Je vais à la gare. I am going to the railway station.
[ʒə ve a la gar]

Je vais (à la) France.
Je vais en France. I am going to France.
[ʒə ve ɑ̃ frɑ̃s]

Verbs

pleuvoir

Il pleut It rains/It's raining
[ill plø]

Lesson 9

At the railway station | *A la gare*

Paul: Good morning Sir. Three tickets for Nice, please.	Paul: Bonjour, monsieur. Je voudrais deux billets pour Nice, s'il vous plaît. [bɔ̃ʒur məsjø ʒə vudre dø bijɛ pur nis sil vu plɛ]
Booking Clerk: For which date ?	L'employé: Pour quelle date? [pur kɛl dat]
Paul: We are leaving on the 3rd July.	Paul: Nous partons le 3 juillet. [nu partɔ̃ lə trwa ʒɥijɛ]
Booking Clerk: Smoking or no smoking compartment?	L'employé: Qu'est-ce que vous désirez: fumeur ou non fumeur ? [kɛskə vu dezire fymœr u nɔ̃ fymœr]
Paul: No smoking compartment.	Paul: Non fumeur. [nɔ̃ fymœr]

Booking Clerk: Here you go.	L.employé: Voilà vos billets. [vwala vo bijɛ]
Paul: Thank you! Do you accept credit cards?	Paul: Merci! Vous prenez les cartes de crédit ? [mɛrsi vu prəne le kart də kredi]
Booking Clerk: Yes, of course. We accept credit cards.	L'employé: Oui, bien sûr. Nous prenons les cartes de crédit. [wi bjɛ̃ syr nu prənɔ̃ le kart də kredi]

Vocabulaire	*Vocabulary*
le billet (n.m.) [lə bije]	ticket
l'employé (n.m.) [lã plwaje]	clerk, employee
la carte (n.f.) [la kart]	card
la cart de credit (n.f.) [la kart də kredi]	credit card
le compartiment fumeur (n.m.) [lə kɔ̃partimã fymœr]	smoking compartment
le compartiment non fumeur (n.m.) [lə kɔ̃partimã nɔ̃ fymœr]	no smoking compartment
bien sûr [bjɛ̃ syr]	of course
désirer (v) [desire]	to want to/ to wish for

<u>Grammaire</u> <u>Grammar</u>

❖ *Before dates , we always use 'le'.*

Examples:

Je pars de Delhi le 3 juillet, 2009. [ʒə par də də li lə trwa ʒɥijɛ dø mil nœf]	I am leaving Delhi on 3rd July, 2009.
Je suis né le 3 mars, 1980. [ʒə sɥi ne lə trwa mars mil nœf sãkatrəvɛ̃]	I was born on 3rd March, 1980.

❖ *Before days, we don.t use any article or preposition.*

Examples:

Je pars de Delhi lundi. [ʒə par də dɛli lœ̃ di]	I am leaving Delhi on Monday.
Je suis né vendredi. [ʒə sɥ i ne vãdrədi]	I was born on Friday.

❖ *Before Months, we use 'en'.*

Example:

Je pars de Delhi en Mars. [ʒə par də dɛli ã mars]	I am leaving Delhi in March.

❖ *Before years, we put 'en'.*

Examples:

Je pars de Delhi en 2009. [ʒə par də dɛli ã dø mil nœf]	I am leaving Delhi in 2009.

Je suis né en 1980.	I was born in 1980.
[ʒə sɥi ne ã mil nœf sã katrəvɛ̃]	

Verbs

désirer

je désire	I want/I wish
[ʒə dezir]	
tu désires	you want/you wish
[ty dezir]	
il désire	he wants/he wishes
[il dezir]	
elle désire	she wants/she wishes
[ɛl dezir]	
nous désirons	we want/we wish
[nu dezirɔ̃]	
vous désirez	you want/you wish
[vu desire]	
ils désirent	they want/they wish
[il dezir]	
elles désirent	they want/they wish
[ɛl dezir]	

Lesson 10

At the airport — *A l'aeroport*

Employee: Good morning Sir!	L'employé: Bonjour, monsieur! [bɔ̃ʒur məsjø]
Pierre: Good morning. Is there any flight for Lyon on 7th August?	Pierre: Bonjour. Est-ce qu'il y a un vol pour Lyon le 7 août? [bɔ̃ʒur ɛskilja œ̃ vɔl pur ljɔ̃ lə sɛt ut]
Employee: Yes sir. There is a direct flight for Lyon at 8 p.m.	L'employé: Oui monsieur. Il y a un vol direct pour Lyon le 20 heures. [wi məsjø il ja œ̃ vɔl dirɛkt pur ljɔ̃ lə sɛt ut]
Pierre: I would like to reserve a seat for 7th August.	Pierre: Je voudrais reserver une place pour le 7 août. [ʒə vudrɛ rezɛrve yn plas pur lə sɛt ut]

Employee: Here you go, Sir.	L'employé: Voila votre billet, monsieur. [vwala vɔtr bije məsjø]
Pierre: Thank you! What time should I come to the airport?	Pierre: Merci! A quelle heure je dois arriver à l'aéroport ? [mɛrsi a kɛlœr ʒə dwa arive a laerɔpɔr]
Employee: At 6 pm, Sir.	L'employé: A 18 heures, monsieur. [a dizœr məsjø]

Vocabulaire	*Vocabulary*
le vol (n.m.) [lə vɔl]	flight
la place (n.f.) [la plas]	seat
l'aéroport (n.m.) [laerɔpɔr]	airport
direct (adj.) [dirɛkt]	direct
reserver (v) [resɛrve]	to book/to reserve
arriver (v) [arive]	to arrive

Grammaire

Grammar

Il y a ...
[il ja]
The expression 'Il y a' stands for 'there is' or 'there are'. It is always followed by a noun.

Examples:

Il y a un garçon. [il ja œ̃ garsɔ̃]	There is a boy.
Il y a des garçons. [il ja de garsɔ̃]	There are boys.
Il y a une fille. [il jayn fij]	There is a girl.
Il y a des filles. [il ja de fij]	There are girls.
Il y a quatre garçons. [il ja katr garsɔ̃]	There are four boys.
Il y a quatre filles. [il ja katr fij]	There are four girls.

Verbs

reserver

je reserve [ʒə rezɛrv]	I reserve/I am reserving I book/I am booking
tu reserves [ty rezɛrv]	you reserve/you are reserving you book/you are booking
il reserve [il rezɛrv]	he reserves/he is reserving he books/he is booking

elle reserve [ɛl rezɛrv]	she reserves/she is reserving she books/she is booking
nous reservons [nu rezɛrvɔ̃]	we reserve/we are reserving we book/we are booking
vous reservez [vu rezɛrve]	you reserve/you are reserving you book/you are booking.
ils reservent [il rezɛrv]	they reserve/they are reserving they book/they are booking
elles reservent [ɛl rezɛrv]	they reserve/they are reserving they book/they are booking

Example:

Je reserve une place. [ʒe rezɛrv yn plas]	I reserve a seat/I am reserving a seat.

arriver

j'arrive [ʒariv]	I arrive/I am arriving I reach/I am reaching I come/I am coming
tu arrives [ty ariv]	you arrive/you are arriving you reach/you are reaching you come/you are coming
il arrive [ilariv]	he arrives/he is arriving he reaches/he is reaching he comes/he is coming
elle arrive [ɛlariv]	she arrives/she is arriving she reaches/she is reaching she comes/she is coming

nous arrivons [nuzarivɔ̃]	we arrive/we are arriving we reach/we are reaching we come/we are coming
vous arrivez [vuzarive]	you arrive/you are arriving you reach/you are reaching you come/you are coming
ils arrivent [ilzariv]	they arrive/they are arriving they reach/they are reaching they come/they are coming
elles arrivent [ɛlzariv]	they arrive/they are arriving they reach/they are reaching they come/they are coming

❖ *The verb 'arriver' takes the preposition 'à', 'de' or 'chez' depending upon the context.*

Examples:

J'arrive à Delhi. [ʒariv a dɛli]	I reach Delhi/I am reaching Delhi.
J'arrive de Paris. [ʒariv də pari]	I come from Paris/I am coming from Paris.
J'arrive chez Paul. [ʒariv ʃe pɔl]	I reach Paul's place/I am reaching Paul's place. I come to Paul's place/I am coming to Paul's place.

Lesson 11

Hotel — L'hotel

Hotel	L'hotel
Tourist: Good morning. Do you have a room for two days?	Le touriste: Bonjour. Est-ce que vous avez une chambre pour deux jours ? [bɔ̃ʒur ɛskə vuzave yn ʃãbr pur dø ʒur]
Receptionist: You want a double room?	La réceptionniste: Vous voulez une chambre à deux lits ? [vu vule yn ʃãbr a dø li]
Tourist: Yes.	Le touriste: Oui. [wi]
Receptionist: We have a room available on the third floor.	La réceptionniste: Il nous reste une chambre au 3ème étage. [il nu rɛst ynʃãbr o trwaziɛm etaʒ]
Tourist: That's fine. I will take this room. What time is the breakfast served?	Le touriste: C'est très bien. Je vais prendre cette chambre. A quelle heure est le petit déjeuner servi ?

	[sɛ trɛ bjɛ̃ ʒe vɛ prãdr sɛt ʃãbr] [a kɛlœr ɛ lə pəti deʒoene sɛrvi]
Receptionist: Breakfast is served between 8 a.m. and 9 a.m. and dinner between 8 p.m. and 10 p.m.	La réceptionniste: Le petit déjeuner est servi entre 8h et 9h. Le dîner est servi entre 20 h et 22h. [lə pəti deʒœne ɛ sɛrvi ãtr ɥitœr e nœvœr] [lə dine ɛ sɛrvi ãtr vɛ̃toer e vɛ̃t døzœr]
Tourist: That's perfect.	Le touriste: C'est parfait. [sɛ parfɛ]
Receptionist: Every evening, there is a dance performance in the hotel. It starts at 7 p.m. and ends at 8 p.m.	La réceptionniste: Chaque soir, nous avons un spectacle de danse. Il commence à 19 h et finit à 20 h. [ʃak swar nuzavɔ̃ œ̃ spɛktakl də dãs] [il kɔmãs a diznœvœr e fini a vɛ̃tœr]
Tourist: Oh that's great. Thank You	Le touriste: Ah, c'est bien. Merci. [a sɛ bjɛ̃ mɛrsi]

Vocabulaire	Vocabulary
la chambre (n.f.) [laʃãbr]	room
la chamre à deux lits (n.f.) [laʃãbr a dø li]	double room
l'étage (n.m.) [letaʒ]	floor
le spectacle (n.m.) [lə spɛktakl]	show
rester (v) [rɛste]	to remain/to stay
servir (v) [sɛrvir]	to serve
commencer (v) [kɔmãse]	to start
finir (v) [finir]	to finish

Grammaire *Grammar*

Conjugation of 2nd group verbs in the 'présent'

To conjugate a second group verb in the 'présent' we remove the last 'r' from the verb and add the following suffixes:

je	**-s**	**nous**	**-ssons**
tu	**-s**	**vous**	**-ssez**
il	**-t**	**ils**	**-ssent**
elle	**-t**	**ells**	**-ssent**

Let's see some examples:

finir

je finis [ʒə fini]	I finish/I am finishing
tu finis [ty fini]	you finish/you are finishing
il finit [il fini]	he finishes/he is finishing
elle finit [ɛl fini]	she finishes/she is finishing
nous fini**ssons** [nu finisɔ̃]	we finish/we are finishing
vous fini**ssez** [vu finise]	you finish/you are finishing
ils fini**ssent** [il finis]	they finish/they are finishing

elles fini**ssent** [ɛl finis]	they finish/they are finishing

❖ *The verb 'finir' takes 'de' when it's followed by a verb. It does not take any preposition when it is followed by a noun.*

Examples:

Je finis de travailler. [ʒə fini də travaje]	I finish working.
Je finis le travail. [ʒə fini lə travaj]	I finish the work/ I am finishing the work.

Conjugation of some more 2nd group verbs

choisir (to choose)

je choisis [ʒə ʃwazi]	I choose/I am choosing
tu choisis [ty ʃwazi]	you choose/you are choosing
il choisit [il ʃwazi]	he chooses/he is choosing
elle choisit [ɛl ʃwazi]	she chooses/she is choosing
nous choisissons [nu ʃwazisɔ̃]	we choose/we are choosing
vous choisissez [vu ʃwazise]	you choose/you are choosing
ils choisi**ssent**	they choose/they are

[il ʃwazis]　　choosing

elles choisi**ssent** [ɛl ʃwazis]　　they choose/they are choosing

❖ *The verb 'choisir' takes the preposition 'de' when it's followed by a verb. It does not take any preposition if it is followed by a noun.*

Examples:

Je choisis de travailler.　　I choose to work.

[ʒə wazi də travaje]

Je choisis la chemise rouge.　　I choose the red shirt.

[ʒə wazi la əmiz ruʒ]

Some frequently used 2nd group verbs

remplir [r plir]　　to fill

approfondir [apr fɔ̃dir]　　to deepen

grandir [grãdir]　　to grow taller

rougir [rugir]　　to turn red/to blush

blanchir [blãʃir]　　to turn white/to whiten

jaunir [ʒonir]　　to turn yellow

Other Verbs

rester

je reste — I stay/I am staying
[ʒə rɛst]

tu restes — you stay/you are staying
[ty rɛst]

il reste — he stays/he is staying
[il rɛst]

elle reste — she stays/she is staying
[ɛl rɛst]

nous restons — we stay/we are staying
[nu rɛstɔ̃]

vous restez — you stay/you are staying
[vu rɛste]

ils restent — they stay/they are staying
[il rɛst]

elles restent — they stay/they are staying
[ɛl rɛst]

Example:

Je reste chez paul. — I stay at paul's place.
[ʒə rɛst ʃe p l]
ɔ

servir

je sers [ʒə sɛr]	I serve/I am serving
tu sers [ty sɛr]	you serve/you are serving
il sert [il sɛr]	he serves/he is serving
elle sert [ɛl sɛr]	she serves/she is serving
nous servons [nu sɛrvɔ̃]	we serve/we are serving
vous servez [vu sɛrve]	you serve/you are serving
ils servent [il sɛrv]	they serve/they are serving
elles servent [ɛl sɛrv]	they serve/they are serving

❖ *When the verb 'servir' is followed by the name of a dish or a drink, it does not take any preposition.*

Example:

Je sers du thé. — I serve tea/I am serving tea.

[ʒə sɛr dy te]

❖ *If you want to say "I serve tea to Paul" you say: "Je sers du thé à Paul".*

commencer

je commence [ʒə k mãs] ɔ	I start/I am starting
tu commences [ty k mãs] ɔ	you start/you are starting
il commence [il k mãs] ɔ	he starts/he is starting
elle commence [ɛl k mãs] ɔ	she starts/she is starting
nous commençons [nu k mãsɔ̃] ɔ	we start/we are starting
vous commencez [vu k mãse] ɔ	you start/you are starting
ils commencent [il k mãs] ɔ	they start/they are starting
elles commencent [ɛlk mãs] ɔ	they start/they are starting

❖ *The verb 'commencer' does not take any preposition when it is followed by a noun. It takes 'à' when it is followed by a verb.*

Examples:

Je commence le travail. [ʒə k m s lə travaj] ɔ ã	I start the work/I am starting the work.
Je commence à travailler. [ʒə k m s a travaje] ɔ ã	I start working.

Lesson 12

Informal letter *Lettre informelle*

New Delhi, 2nd November, 2007

Dear Shoa,

How are you? I came back from France yesterday. I stayed three weeks in Paris. It's a beautiful city. I also visited Lyon and Nice.

In Paris, I visited almost all the historical monuments and famous places. Eiffel Tower and Arc of Triumph are magnificent. I enjoyed a lot in France.

Best regards

Sara

Chère Shoa,

[ʃɛrʃoa]

Comment ça va? Je suis rentrée de la France hier. J'ai

[kɔmã sa va] [ʒə sɥi rãtre də la frãs jiɛr] [ʒe

passé trois semaines à Paris. C'est une belle ville. J'ai

pase trwa səmɛn a pari] [sɛtyn bɛl vil] [ʒe

aussi visité Lyon et Nice. A Paris, j'ai visité presque tous

osi vizite ljɔ̃ e nis] [a pari ʒe vizite prɛskə tu

les monuments historiques et les endroits célébres. La tour

le mɔnymã istɔrik e lezãdrwa selɛbr] [la tur

Eiffel et l'Arc de Triomphe sont magnifiques. Je me suis

ɛfɛl e larc də trijɔ̃f sɔ̃ maɲifik] [ʒe mə s iɥ

bien amusée en France.

bjɛ̃ namyze ãfrãs]

Bien amicalement

[bjɛ̃ namikalmã]

Sara

[sara]

Vocabulaire	Vocabulary
la lettre (n.f.)	letter
[la lɛtr]	
la semaine (n.f.)	week
[la səmɛn]	
la ville (n.f.)	city/town
[la vil]	
le monument (n.m.)	monuments
[lə mɔnymã]	
l'endroit (n.m.)	place
[lãdrwa]	
historique (adj.)	historical
[istɔrik]	
célèbre (adj.)	famous
[selɛbr]	
belle (adj.f.)	beautiful
[bɛl]	
magnifique (adj.)	magnificent
[maɲifik]	
bien amicalement	yours/best regards
[bjɛ̃ namikalmã]	(in a letter)
passer (v)	to spend
[pase]	
visiter (v)	to visit
[vizite]	
s'amuser (v)	to enjoy oneself
[samyze]	

Passé Composé

The 'Passé Composé' is used to indicate that an action has been completed. Let's see some sentences in the passé composé.

Il a regardé la télévision. — He watched television/
[il a rəgarde la televizjɔ̃] — He has watched television.

Il a parlé à son ami. — He spoke to his friend/
[il a parle a sɔ̃nami] — He has spoken to his friend.

Conjugation of verbs in the 'passé composé'

In order to conjugate a verb in the 'passé composé', we first conjugate the verb 'avoir' in 'présent' and then we add the 'participe passé' of the verb in question.

The 'participe passé' of a first group verb is formed by dropping the last 'r' of the infinitive and adding an 'accent aigu' to the last 'e'.

Let's see the conjugation of some first group verbs:

parler

J'ai parlé — I spoke/I have spoken
[ʒe parle]

tu as parlé — you spoke/you have spoken
[ty a parle]

il a parlé [il a parle]	he spoke/he has spoken
elle a parlé [ɛl a parle]	she spoke/she has spoken
nous avons parlé [nuzavɔ̃ parle]	we spoke/we have spoken
vous avez parlé [vuzave parle]	you spoke/you have spoken
ils ont parlé] [ilzɔ̃ parle]	they spoke/they have spoken
elles ont parlé ɛlzɔ̃ parle]	they spoke/they have spoken

Example:

j'ai parlé à paul. [ʒe parle a pɔl]	I spoke to Paul/ I have spoken to Paul.

passer

j'ai passé [ʒe pase]	I spent/I have spent
tu as passé [ty a pase]	you spent/you have spent
il a passé [il a pase]	he spent/he has spent
elle a passé [ɛl a pase]	she spent/she has spent
nous avons passé [nuzavɔ̃ pase]	we spent/we have spent

vous avez passé	you spent/you have spent
[vuzave pase]	
ils ont passé	they spent/they have spent
[ilzɔ̃ pase]	
elles ont passé	they spent/they have spent
[ɛlzɔ̃ pase]	

Example:

J'ai passé deux jours à Paris.	I spent two days in Paris/
[ʒe pase dø ʒur a pari]	I have spent two days in Paris.

visiter

j'ai visité	I visited/I have visited
[ʒe vizite]	
tu as visité	you visited/you have visited
[ty a vizite]	
il a visité	he visited/he has visited
[il a vizite]	
elle a visité	she visited/she has visited
[ɛl a vizite]	
nous avons visité	we visited/we have visited
[nuzavɔ̃ vizite]	
vous avez visité	you visited/you have visited
[vuzave vizite]	
ils ont visité	they visited/they have visited
[ilzɔ̃ vizite]	
elles ont visité	they visited/they have visited
[ɛlzɔ̃ vizite]	

Example:

J'ai visité la tour Eiffel.	I visited Eiffel Tower/
[ʒe vizite la tur ɛfɛl]	I have visited Eiffel Tower.

❖ ***The majority of verbs are conjugated with 'avoir' in the 'passé composé'. But the following verbs are conjugated with 'être'.***

devenir [dəvnir]	to become
rentrer [rãtre]	to return
monter [mɔ̃te]	to climb/to go up
rester [rɛste]	to stay
sortir [sɔrtir]	to go out/to come out
venir [vənir]	to come
aller [ale]	to go
naître [nɛtr]	to be born
descendre [dəsãdr]	to come down/to get down

entrer [ãtre]	to enter
tomber [tɔ̃ be]	to fall
retourner [rəturne]	to come back
arriver [arrive]	to reach/to arrive/to come
mourir [murir]	to die
partir [partir]	to leave
passer [pase]	to go past

- ***To conjugate these verbs, we first conjugate 'être' in the 'présent' and then we add the 'participe passé of the verb in question.***

- ***The 'participe passé' of these verbs agrees in number and gender with the subject with which the verb is used. In other words, we add an 'e' to the 'participe passé' if the subject is feminine and we add an 's', if the subject is plural.***

Let's see some examples:

devenir (participe passé – devenu)

je suis devenu (m.s.) [ʒe sɥi dəvny]	I became/I have become
je suis devenue (f.s.) [ʒe sɥi dəvny]	I became/I have become
tu es devenu (m.s.) [ty ɛ dəvny]	you became/you have become
tu es devenue (f.s.) [ty ɛ dəvny]	you became/you have become
il est devenu (m.s.) [il ɛ dəvny]	he became/he has become
elle est devenue (f.s.) [ɛl ɛ dəvny]	she became/she has become
nous sommes devenus (m.p.) [nu sɔm dəvny]	we became/we have become
nous sommes devenues (f.p.) [nu sɔm dəvny]	we became/we have become
vous êtes devenu (m.s.) [vuzɛt dəvny]	you became/you have become
vous êtes devenue (f.s.) [vuzɛt dəvny]	you became/you have become
vous êtes devenus (m.p.) [vuzɛt dəvny]	you became/you have become
vous êtes devenues (f.p.) [vuzɛt dəvny]	you became/you have become
ils sont devenus (m.p.) [il sɔ̃ dəvny]	they became/they have become
elles sont devenues (f.p.) [ɛl sɔ̃ dəvny]	they became/they have become

Examples:

Je suis devenu un acteur. [ʒe sɥi dəvny œ̃ naktoer]	I became an actor/I have become an actor.
Je suis devenue une actrice. [ʒe sɥi dəvny ynaktris]	I became an actress/ I have become an actress.

<u>aller (participe passé- allé)</u>

je suis allé (m.s.) [ʒe sɥizale]	I went/I have gone
je suis allée (f.s.) [ʒe sɥizale]	I went/have gone
tu es allé (m.s.) [ty ɛ ale]	you went/you have gone
tu es allée (f.s.) [ty ɛ ale]	you went/you have gone
il est allé (m.s.) [ilɛ tale]	he went/he has gone
elle est allée (f.s.) [ɛlɛ tale]	she went/she has gone
nous sommes allés(m.p.) [nu sɔmzale]	we went/we have gone
nous sommes allées (f.p.) [nu sɔmzale]	we went/we have gone
vous êtes allé (m.s.) [vuzetzale]	you went/you have gone
vous êtes allée (f.s.) [vuzetzale]	you went/you have gone

vous êtes allés (m.p.) [vuzetzale] — you went/you have gone

vous êtes allées (f.p.) [vuzetzale] — you went/you have gone

ils sont allés (m.p.) [il sɔ̃tale] — they went/they have gone

elles sont allées (f.p.) [ɛl sɔ̃tale] — they went/they have gone

Example:

Je suis allé au cinema. [ʒe sɥ izale o sinema] — I went to cinema/ I have gone to cinema.

❖ *Reflexive verbs are also conjugated with 'être' in the 'passé composé'.*

Let's see some examples:

<u>s'amuser (participe passé- amusé)</u>

je me suis amusé (m.s.) [ʒə mə sɥ i zamyze] — I enjoyed myself/ I have enjoyed myself

je me suis amusée (f.s.) [ʒə mə sɥ i zamyze] — I have enjoyed myself I enjoyed myself/

Tu t'es amusé (m.s.) [ty tɛ amyze] — you enjoyed yourself/ you have enjoyed yourself

tu t'es amusée (f.s.) [ty tɛ amyze] — you enjoyed yourself/ you have enjoyed yourself

il s.est amusé (m.s.) [il sɛ tamyze] — he enjoyed himself/ he has enjoyed himself

elle s'est amusée (f.s.) [ɛl sɛtamyze]	she enjoyed herself/she has enjoyed herself
Nous nous sommes amusés (m.p.) [nu nu sɔ mzamyze]	we enjoyed ourselves/we have enjoyed ourselves
nous nous sommes amusées (f.p.) [nu nu sɔ mzamyze]	we enjoyed ourselves/we have enjoyed ourselves
vous vous êtes amusé (m.s.) [vu vu zɛtzamyze]	you enjoyed yourself/you have enjoyed yourself
vous vous êtes amusée (f.s.) [vu vu zɛtzamyze]	you enjoyed yourself/you have enjoyed yourself
vous vous êtes amusés (m.p.) [vu vu zɛtzamyze]	you enjoyed yourselves/you have enjoyed yourselves
vous vous êtes amusées (f.p.) [vu vu zɛtzamyze]	you enjoyed yourselves/you have enjoyed yourselves
ils se sont amusés (m.p.) [il sə sɔ̃ tamyze]	they enjoyed themselves/they have enjoyed themselves
elles se sont amusées (f.p.) [ɛl sə sɔ̃tamyze]	they enjoyed themselves/they have enjoyed themselves

Lesson 13

How to talk about your childhood — *Comment parler de votre enfance*

Mr. Vincent: Sir, how long have you been living in Delhi?	M. Vincent: Depuis combien de temps habites-tu à Delhi ? [dəpɥi kɔ̃bjɛ̃ də tã abit ty a dɛli]
Mr. Singh: For the last 40 years.	M. Singh: Depuis 40 ans. [dəpɥi karãtã]
Mr. Vincent: Where did you spend your childhood?	M. Vincent: Où as-tu passé ton enfance? [u a ty pase tɔ̃nãfãs]
Mr. Singh: In Patna.	Mr. Singh: A Patna. [a pətna]
Mr. Vincent: You don't miss your childhood?	Mr. Vincent: Ton enfance ne te manque pas ? [tɔ̃nãfãs nə tə mãk pa]
Mr. Singh: Oh, I miss my childhood a lot. You know, I used to enjoy a lot during	M. Singh: Ah, mon enfance me manque beaucoup. Tu sais, je m'amusais

my childhood. I had many friends. I used to play with them. I used to see movies with them. I was very mischievous. I used to fight with my sisters every day.

beaucoup pendant mon enfance. J'avais plusieurs amis. Je jouais avec eux. Je voyais les films avec eux. J'étais très méchant. Je me battais avec ma soeur tous les jours. [a mɔ̃nãfãs mə mãk boku] [ty sɛ ʒə mamyze boku pãdã mɔ̃nãfãs] [ʒavɛ plysjoer zami] [ʒə ʒuɛ avɛk ø] [ʒə vwajɛ le film avɛk ø] [ʒetɛ trɛ me ʃã] [ʒ mə batɛ avɛk ma soer tu le ʒur]

Vocabulaire	*Vocabulary*
l'enfance (n.f.) [lãfãs]	childhood
méchant (adj. mas.) [meʃã]	mischievous
méchante (adj. fem.) [meʃãt]	mischievous
depuis (prep.) [dəpɥi]	since / for
pendant (prep.) [pãdã]	during
passer (v) [pase]	to spend
savoir (v) [savwar]	to know
se batter (v) [sə batr]	to fight

L'imparfait

The 'imparfait' is used to describe:

- *actions going on in the past.*

Example:

Il jouait au cricket. He was playing cricket.

[il ʒue o kriket]

- *repeated actions in the past.*

Example:

Il jouait au cricket tous les jours. He used to play cricket everyday.

[il ʒue o kriket tu le ʒur]

- *a person, place or circumstances in the past.*

Example:

Il faisait chaud hier. It was hot yesterday.

[il fɛsɛ ʃo ijɛr]

Conjugation of verbs in the 'imparfait'

To conjugate a verb in the 'imparfait', we conjugate the verb with 'nous'in the 'present', remove '-ons' and add the following suffixes.

je	**-ais**	**nous**	**-ions**
tu	**-ais**	**vous**	**-iez**
il	**-ait**	**ils**	**-aient**
elle	**-ait**	**elles**	**-aient**

Let's see some examples:

parler

parlons (conjugation of the verb with nous in the 'présent') - **parl**

je parl**ais** [ʒə parlɛ]	I was speaking/I used to speak
tu parl**ais** [ty parlɛ]	you were speaking/you used to speak
il parl**ait** [il parlɛ]	he was speaking/he used to speak
elle parl**ait** [ɛl parlɛ]	she was speaking/she used to speak
nous parl**ions** [nu parljɔ̃]	we were speaking/we used to speak
vous par**liez** [vu parlje]	you were speaking/you used to speak
ils parl**aient** [il parlɛ]	they were speaking/they used to speak
elles parl**aient** [ɛl parlɛ]	they were speaking/they used to speak

Example:

Je parlais français. [ʒə parlɛ frãsɛ]	I was speaking French/I used to speak French.

finir

finissons (conjugation of the verb with nous in the 'présent'.)
- finiss

je finissais [ʒə finisɛ]	I was finishing/I used to finish
tu finissais [ty finisɛ]	you were finishing/you used to finish
il finissait [il finisɛ]	he was finishing/he used to finish
elle finissait [ɛl finisɛ]	she was finishing/she used to finish
nous finissions [nu finisjɔ̃]	we were finishing/we used to finish
vous finissiez [vu finisje]	you were finishing/you used to finish
ils finissaient [il finisɛ]	they were finishing/they used to finish
elles finissaient [ɛl finisɛ]	they were finishing/they used to finish

Example:

Je finissais mon devoir. [ʒə finisɛ mɔ̃ dəvwar]	I was finishing my home work/ I used to finish my homework.

passer

passons (conjugation of the verb with 'nous' in the 'présent')
- pass

je passais [ʒə pasɛ]	I was spending/I used to spend
tu passais [ty pasɛ]	you were spending/you used to spend
il passait [il pasɛ]	he was spending/he used to spend
elle passait [ɛl pasɛ]	she was spending/she used to spend
nous passions [nu pasjɔ̃]	we were spending/we used to spend
vous passiez [vu pasje]	you were spending/you used to spend
ils passaient [il pasɛ]	they were spending/they used to spend
elles passaient [ɛl pasɛ]	they were spending/they used to spend

Example:

Je passais mes week-ends [ʒə pasɛ me wikɛnd	I used to spend my weekend
avec mes parents quand avɛk me parã kã	with my parents when
j'étais étudiant. ʒetɛ zetydjã]	I was a student.

savoir

savons (conjugation of the verb with 'nous' in the 'présent') - **sav**

je savais [ʒə savɛ]	I knew
tu savais [ty savɛ]	you knew
il savait [il savɛ]	he knew
elle savait [ɛl savɛ]	she knew
nous savions [nu savjɔ̃]	we knew
vous saviez [vu savje]	you knew
ils savaient [il savɛ]	they knew
elles savaient [ɛl savɛ]	they knew

Example:

Je savais parler français. [ʒə savɛ parle frɑ̃sɛ]	I knew how to speak French.

❖ *All verbs are conjugated according to this pattern except the verb 'être'.*

<u>être</u>

j'étais [ʒetɛ]	I was/I used to be
tu étais [ty etɛ]	you were/you used to be
il était [il etɛ]	he was/he used to be
elle était [ɛl etɛ]	she was/she used to be
nous étions [nuzetjɔ̃]	we were/we used to be
vous étiez [vuzetje]	you were/you used to be
ils étaient [ilzetɛ]	they were/they used to be
elles étaient [ɛlzetɛ]	they were/they used to be

Example:

J'étais très méchant [ʒetɛ trɛ meʃã	I was very mischievous
pendant mon enfance. pãdã mɔ̃nãfãs]	during my childhood.

Conjugation of reflexive verbs in the 'imparfait'

se battre

battons (conjugation of the verb with 'nous' in the 'présent') – **batt**

je me battais [ʒə mə batɛ]	I used to fight (with sb.)/ I was fighting (with sb.)
tu te battais [ty tə batɛ]	you used to fight (with sb.)/ you were fighting (with sb.)
il se battait [il sə batɛ]	he used to fight (with sb.)/ he was fighting (with sb.)
elle se battait [ɛl sə batɛ]	she used to fight (with sb.)/ she was fighting (with sb.)
nous nous battions [nu nu batjɔ̃]	we used to fight (with sb.)/ we were fighting (with sb.)
vous vous battiez [vu vu batje]	you used to fight (with sb.)/ you were fighting (with sb.)
ils se battaient [il sə batɛ]	they used to fight (with sb.)/ they were fighting (with sb.)
elles se battaient [ɛl sə batɛ]	they used to fight (with sb.)/ they were fighting (with sb.)

Lesson 14

Email — *Le couriel*

Subject: Your mail
Date: Monday, June 16, 2008.
From: ryankhan@yahoo.com
To: pierre07@rediffmail.com

Hi Pierre,

I received your mail yesterday. I am happy to know that your vacation is starting from the 25th June. Mine is commencing form the 21st June. This time, I am not going back home. I will stay in Paris. So I invite you to spend your vacation with me. It will be a great fun. We will go to cinema and disco every day.

I hope you will accept my invitation.

See you soon.

Yours
Ryan

Objet:	Ton message
[bʒə]	[t ɔ̃mesaʒ]
Date:	Lundi, 16 Juin, 2008.
[dat]	[lœ̃di sɛz ʒɥɛ̃dø milɥit]
De :	ryankhan@yahoo.com
[də]	
A :	pierre07@rediffmail.com
[a]	

Bonjour Pierre!
[bɔ̃ʒur pjɛr]
J'ai bien reçu ton message hier. Je suis content
[ʒe bjɛ rəsy tɔ̃ mesaʒ ijɛr] [ʒə sɥi kɔ̃tã
d'apprendre que tes vacances commencent le 25 Juin. Mes
daprãdr kə te vakãs kɔmãs lə vɛ̃t sɛ̃k ʒɥɛ̃] [me
vacances commencent le 21 Juin. Cette fois, je ne rentre
vakãs kɔmãs lə vɛ̃t eœ̃ʒɥɛ̃] [sɛt fwa ʒə nə rãtr
pas chez mois. Je resterai à Paris. Alors, Je t'invite à
paʃe mwa] [ʒə rɛstəre a pari] [alɔr ʒə tɛ̃vit a
passer tes vacances avec moi. Nous nous amuserons
pase te vakãs avɛk mwa] [nu nu zamyzrɔ̃
beaucoup. Nous irons au cinéma et à la disco tous les
boku] [nu zirɔ̃ o sinema e a la disko tu le
jours. J'espère que tu accepteras mon invitations.
ʒur] [ʒɛspɛr kə ty aksɛptəra mɔ̃nɛ̃vitasjɔ̃]

A bientôt.
[a bjɛ̃to]

Amicalement
[amikalmã]
Ryan

Vocabulaire	*Vocabulary*
le message (n.m.) [ləmesaʒ]	message
les vacances (n.f.) [le vakãs]	vacation
la disco/la discothèque (n.f.) [la disko] [la diskotɛk]	disco
content (adj.m.) [kɔ̃tã]	happy
contente (adj.f.) [kɔ̃tãt]	happy
inviter (v) [ɛ̃vite]	to invite
espérer (v) [ɛspere]	to hope
accepter (v) [aksɛpte]	to accept

Le futur

The 'futur' is used to describe an action which will occur in future.

Examples:

Je jouerai au cricket. I will play cricket.

[ʒə ʒuere o krikɛt]

Je finirai mon devoir à l'heure. I will finish my homework in time.

[ʒə finire mɔ̃ dəvwar a lœr]

Conjugation of regular verbs in 'futur'

To conjugate a regular verb ending in 'er' or 'ir', we take the infinitive form of the verb and add the following suffixes:

je	**- ai**	**nous**	**-ons**
tu	**- as**	**vous**	**-ez**
il	**-a**	**ils**	**-ont**
elle	**-a**	**elles**	**-ont**

To conjugate a verb ending in 're', we take the infinitive form of the verb, remove the last 'e' and add the above suffixes.

Let's see some examples:

inviter

j'inviterai [ʒɛ̃vitəre]	I will invite
tu inviteras [ty ɛ̃vitəra]	you will invite
il invitera [il ɛ̃vitəra]	he will invite
elle invitera [ɛl ɛ̃vitəra]	she will invite
nous inviterons [nuzɛ̃vitərɔ̃]	we will invite
vous inviterez [vuzɛ̃vitəre]	you will invite
ils inviteront [ilzɛ̃vitərɔ̃]	they will invite
elles inviteront [ɛlzɛ̃vitərɔ̃]	they will invite

Example:

J'inviterai mon ami à passer ses vacances avec moi. [ʒɛ̃ vitəre mɔ̃nami a pase se vakɑ̃s avɛk mwa]	I will invite my friend to spend his vacation with me.

accepter

j'accepterai [ʒaksɛptəre]	I will accept
tu accepteras [ty aksɛptəra]	you will accept
il acceptera [il aksɛptəra]	he will accept
elle acceptera [ɛl aksɛptəra]	she will accept
nous accepterons [nuzaksɛptərɔ̃]	we will accept
vous accepterez [vuzaksɛptəre]	you will accept
ils accepteront [ilzaksɛptərɔ̃]	they will accept
elles accepteront [ɛlzaksɛptərɔ̃]	they will accept

Examples:

J'accepterai son invitation. I will accept his invitation.
[ʒaksɛptəre sɔ̃nɛ̃vitasjɔ̃]

J'accepterai de jouer avec lui. I will accept to play with him.
[ʒaksɛptəre də ʒwe avɛk lɥ i]

se laver (to take a bath)

je me laverai [ʒə mə lavəre]	I will take a bath
tu te laveras [ty tə lavəra]	you will take a bath
il se lavera [il sə lavəra]	he will take a bath
elle se lavera [ɛl sə lavəra]	she will take a bath
nous nous laverons [nu nu lavərɔ̃]	we will take a bath
vous vous laverez [vu vu lavəre]	you will take a bath
ils se laveront [il sə lavərɔ̃]	they will take a bath
elles se laveront ɛl se laverɔ̃]	they will take a bath

Conjugation of some irregular verbs in 'futur'

être

je serai [ʒə sərɛ]	I will have
tu seras [ty səra]	you will have
il sera [il səra]	he will be
elle sera [ɛl səra]	she will be
nous serons [nu sərɔ̃]	we will be
vous serez [vu səre]	you will be
ils seront [il sərɔ̃]	they will be
elles seront [ɛl sərɔ̃]	they will be

avoir

J'aurai [ʒɔrɛ]	I will be
tu auras [ty ɔra]	you will be

il aura [il ɔra]	he will have
elle aura [ɛl ɔra]	she will have
nous aurons [nu zɔrɔ̃]	we will have
vous aurez [vu zɔre]	you will have
ils auront [il zɔrɔ̃]	they will have
elles auront [ɛl zɔrɔ̃]	they will have

aller

j'irai [ʒirɛ]	I will go
tu iras [ty ira]	you will go
il ira [il ira]	he will go
elle ira [ɛl ira]	she will go
nous irons [nu zirɔ̃]	we will go
vous irez [vu zire]	you will go

ils iront [il zirɔ̃]	they will go
elles iront [ɛl zirɔ̃]	they will go

venir

je viendrai [ʒə viɛ̃drɛ]	I will come
tu viendras [ty viɛ̃dra]	you will come
il viendra [il viɛ̃dra]	he will come
elle viendra [ɛl viɛ̃dra]	she will come
nous viendrons [nu viɛ̃drɔ̃]	we will come
vous viendrez [vu viɛ̃dre]	you will come
ils viendront [il viɛ̃drɔ̃]	they will come
elles viendront [ɛl viɛ̃drɔ̃]	they will come

ADDITIONAL VOCABULARY

Ordinal numbers

1e	premier (m) / première (f) [prəmjɛr]	first
2ème	deuxième [døzjɛm]	second
3ème	troisième [trwazjɛm]	third
4ème	quatrième [katrjɛm]	fourth
5ème	cinquième [sɛ̃kjɛm]	fifth
6ème	sixième [sizjɛm]	sixth
7ème	septième [sɛtjɛm]	seventh
8ème	huitième [itjɛm]	eighth
9ème	neuvième [nœvjɛm]	ninth
10ème	dixième [dizjɛm]	tenth
11ème	onzième [ɔ̃zjɛm]	eleventh

12ème	douzième [duzjɛm]	twelth
13ème	treizième [trɛzjɛm]	thirteenth
14ème	quatorzième [katɔrzjɛm]	fourteenth
15ème	quinzième [kɛ̃zjɛm]	fifteenth
16ème	seizième [sɛzjɛm]	sixteenth
17ème	dix-septième [disɛtjɛm]	seventeenth
18ème	dix-huitième [dizɥitjɛm]	eighteenth
19ème	dix-neuvième [diznœvjɛm]	nineteenth
20ème	vingtème [vɛ̃tjɛm]	twentieth

Professions

le professeur — professor
[lə prɔfɛsœr]

le médecin — doctor
[lə medsɛ̃]

l'écrivain — writer
[lekrivɛ̃]

le mécanicien — mechanic
[lə mekanisjɛ̃]

le fonctionnaire — civil servant
[lə fɔ̃ ksjɔnɛ r]

le commerçant — shopkeeper
[lə kɔmɛrsã]

l'ingénieur — engineer
[lɛ̃genjœr]

l'architecte — architect
[lar itɛkt]

le journaliste — journalist (male)
[lə ʒ urnalist]

la journaliste — journalist (female)
[la ʒurnalist]

le secrétaire — secretary (male)
[lə səkretɛr]

la secrétaire — secretary (female)
[la səkretɛr]

l'étudiant — student (male)
[letydjã]

l'étudiante [letydjãt]	student (female)
le musician [ləmyzisjɛ̃]	musician (male)
la musicienne [lamyzisjɛn]	musician (female)
le chanteur [ləʃãtœr]	singer (male)
la chanteuse [laʃãtøz]	singer (female)
l'homme d'affaires [lɔm dafɛr]	businessman
la femme d'affaires [la fam dafɛr]	business woman

Means of transport

le train [lə trɛ̃]	train
l'avion [lavjɔ̃]	aeroplane
le bateau [lə bato]	ship
l'autobus [lotɔbys]	bus
la voiture [la vwatyr]	car
le taxi [lə taksi]	taxi
la moto [la mɔto]	motorbike
le vélo [lə velo]	bicycle
la bicyclette [la bisiklɛt]	bicycle
l'auto [lotɔ]	auto rickshaw
le cycle-pousse [lə sikl pus]	cycle rickshaw
le metro [lə mɛtro]	metro
le tram [lə tram]	tram
le camion [lə kamjɔ̃]	truck

Electronic gadgets

la télévision [la televizjɔ̃]	television
la radio [la radjo]	radio
la magnétophone [la maɳetɔfɔn]	tape recorder
le portable [lə portabl]	mobile phone
le telephone [lə telefɔn]	telephone
l'ordinateur [lɔrdinatœr]	computer
la calculatrice [lã kalkylatris]	calculator
l'appareil photo [laparɛj fɔto]	camera (for still photos)
la camera [lã kamera]	camera (for video)
la montre [la mɔ̃tr]	watch
l'horloge [lɔrlɔʒ]	clock
le réveil [lə revɛj]	alarm clock
l'écouteur [lekutœr]	earphone
le baladeur [lə baladœr]	walkman

Countries and nationalities

Countries	**Les pays**	**Nationalities**	**Les nationalités**
Scotland	L'Écosse (f) [lekɔs]	Scottish	écossais (m) écossaise (f)
Norway	la Norvège (f) [la nɔrvɛʒ]	Norwegian	norvégien (m) norvégienne (f)
Sweden	la Suède (f) [la swɛd]	Swedish	suédois (m) suédoise (f)
Mexico	la Mexique (m) [la mɛksik]	Mexican	méxicain (m) méxicaine (f)
Denmark	le Danemark (m) [lə danmark]	Danish	denois (m) denoise (f)
Algeria	l'Algérie (f) [lalʒeri]	Algerian	algérien (m) algérienne (f)
The Netherlands	les Pays-Bas (m) [le pɛjba]	Dutch	hollondais (m) hollandaise (f)
Austria	l'Austriche (f) [lostriʃ]	Austrian	austrichien (m) austrichienne (f)
Finland	la Finlande (f) [la finlãd]	Finnish	finlandais (m) finlandaise (f)
Poland	la Pologne (f) [la p ɹ ɔɳ]	Polish	polonais (m) polonaise (f)
Australia	l'Australie (f) [lostrali]	Australian	australien (m) australienne (f)
Mauritius	l'ile Maurice (f) [lil moris]	Mauritian	mauricien (m) mauricienne (f)

Languages

le français [lə frɑ̃sɛ]	French
l'anglais [lɑ̃glɛ]	English
le hindi [lə indi]	Hindi
l'ourdou [lurdu]	Urdu
la perse [la pɛrs]	Persian
l'arabe [larab]	Arabic
l'espagnole [lɛspaɳɔl]	Spanish
l'allemand [lalmɔ̃]	German
le chinois [ləʃinwa]	Chinese
la russe [la rys]	Russian
l'italien [litaljɛ̃]	Italien
le japonais [lə ʒapɔnɛ]	Japanese

le sanskrit [lə sãskri]	Sanskrit
le coréen [lə kɔreɛ̃]	Korean
le portugais [lə pɔrtygɛ]	Portuguese
le latin [lə latɛ̃]	Latin
le néerlandais [lə neɛrlãdɛ]	Dutch

Food

du pain (m) [dy pɛ̃]	bread
du lait (m) [dy lɛ]	milk
du beurre (m) [dy bœr]	butter
du ris (m) [dy ri]	rice
du poulet (m) [dy pulɛ]	chicken
du mouton (m) [dy mutɔ̃]	mutton
du boeuf (m) [dy bœf]	beef
du gâteau (m) [dy gato]	cake
du poisson (m) [dy pwasɔ̃]	fish
l'œuf (m) [lœf]	egg
du sucre (m) [dy sykr]	sugar
du sel (m) [dy sɛl]	salt

de la glace (f) [də la glas]	ice cream
du chocolat (m) [dy ʃɔ kɔla]	chocolate
du thé (m) [dy te]	tea
du café (m) [dy kafe]	coffee
du jus de fruit (m) [dy ʒy də frɥi]	fruit juice
du vin (m) [dy vɛ̃]	wine
de l'eau (f) [də lo]	water
du fromage (m) [dy frɔmaʒ]	cheese

Fruits

l'orange (f) [lɔrɑ̃ʒ]	orange
la mangue (f) [la m ɑ̃ g]	mango
la banane (f) [la banan]	banana
l'ananas (m) [lanana]	pineapple
la papaye (f) [la papaj]	papaya
la goyave (f) [la gɔjav]	guava
la pomme (f) [la pɔm]	apple
la grenade (f) [la grənad]	pomegranate
le raisin (m) [lə rɛsɛ̃]	grapes
la noix de coco (f) [la nwa də kɔkɔ]	coconut
la cerise (f) [la səriz]	cherry
la fraise (f) [la frɛz]	strawberry

Sports

Le cricket : Cricket
[lə krikɛt]

Le football : Football
[lə futbol]

Le tennis : Tennis
[lə tenis]

Le tennis de table : Table tennis
[lə tenis də tabl]

Le badminton : badminton
[lə badmint n]

Le basket: Basketball
[lə baskɛt]

Le Volley-ball: Volleyball
[lə v lɛbol]

La natation : Swimming
[la natasj]

Le cyclisme: Cycling
[lə siklism]

Le rugby : Rugby
[lə rygbi]